# THE WAH-WAH DIARIES

## THE MAKING OF A FILM

# RICHARD E. GRANT

PICADOR

First published 2006 by Picador

First published in paperback 2006 by Picador

This edition published 2006 by Picador
an imprint of Pan Macmillan, a division of Macmillan Publishers Limited
Pan Macmillan, 20 New Wharf Road, London N1 9RR
Basingstoke and Oxford
Associated companies throughout the world
www.panmacmillan.com

ISBN 978-0-330-44197-1

3 5 7 9 8 6 4

A CIP catalogue record for this book is available from
the British Library.

Printed and bound by CPI Group (UK) Ltd, Croydon, CR0 4YY

Visit www.picador.com to read more about all our books
and to buy them. You will also find features, author interviews and
news of any author events, and you can sign up for e-newsletters
so that you're always first to hear about our new releases.

*For my wife and daughter – beyond all beyond*

# Cast List

| | |
|---|---|
| GABRIEL BYRNE | Harry Compton |
| MIRANDA RICHARDSON | Lauren Compton |
| ZAC FOX | Young Ralph Compton |
| NICHOLAS HOULT | Teenage Ralph Compton |
| EMILY WATSON | Ruby Compton |
| JULIE WALTERS | Gwen Traherne |
| IAN ROBERTS | John Traherne |
| JULIAN WADHAM | Charles |
| FENELLA WOOLGAR | June |
| JOHN MATSHIKIZA | Dr Zim Mzimba |
| SIBUSISO MAMBA | Father Ndlovu |
| SINDISISWE NXUMALO | Regina |
| MATHOKOZA SIBIYU | Dozen |
| MICHAEL RICHARDS | Tobias |
| CELIA IMRIE | Lady Riva Hardwick |
| JOHN CARLISLE | Sir Gifford Hardwick |
| SID MITCHELL | Vernon |
| OLIVIA GRANT | Monica |
| CAROLINE SMART | Taj |
| KIM BORRELL | Bunny |
| CLARE MARSHALL | Box office manageress |
| TONY HATTON | Mr Parker |

# DEVELOPMENT

## 14 October 1999

The Ivy, London. The producer Hilary Heath has invited me for lunch to discuss possible projects. Having assumed she is aware of the idea for a screenplay I have been blathering about writing for some years, I believe this to be the meeting at which I am required to deliver my 'pitch'. Not at all – Hilary thinks I might have a novel I am interested in adapting, or some such. Tall, beautiful, impulsive and unfazed, she accommodates my tangential idea and clucks welcome noises of enthusiasm when I suggest spooling forth the synopsis between mouthfuls of Caesar salad.

It goes something like this: 'Coming of age at the end of an age story set in Africa during the last gasp of Empire, circa 1969, about a man in his mid-forties, facing the premature end of his colonial career due to imminent Independence and, cuckolded by his wife, left to bring up their eleven-year-old son. Meanwhile the expat community stake their claim in the coming Independence celebrations by mounting an amateur production of *Camelot* to entertain the visiting British royal coming out to officiate at the handover. A comic drama. Purely autobiographical and as true as fiction.'

'Sounds wonderful – have you got a script?'

'Well, yes, but not quite. It's in a thousand pieces. Notes on napkins, on scraps of paper in drawers and plastic bags, old theatre programmes . . . But I do have a structure and a list of scenes.'

'How long will you need to write up a first draft?' Hilary has an uncompromisingly direct approach, accompanied by a sort of nervy, skittish quality that can sound either accusatory or blunt, or both.

I suppose I had been waiting for someone to demand a draft for years, but when finally asked the direct question, I'm not really prepared for it. Somehow I convinced myself it would never happen.

'Couple of months,' eases its way past my lips, which clearly know something the rest of me doesn't.

'How about aiming for just this side of Christmas, so I can read it on holiday in Barbados?'

'Sounds good to me,' I say, which should have *quavered* forth, but no, the words come out sounding quite assured and emphatic as I chew heartily, trying to hide the fact from all my panic stations that red alert might be a mere pudding away.

Before I know it, Hilary is my appointed producer and I leave lunch as her appointed writer-director.

I allowed myself a momentary auteur hop, skip and a scramble down the escalators into Leicester Square station and sat all the way home looking at my fellow travellers wondering whether they too were full of secret plans and subsidized lunch. 'But you haven't even written it up properly yet,' said my wife, only just managing to suppress a hearty snort.

'I know, but I'm going to.'

In my study I groaned and rummaged my way through every box, bag and briefcase to collect all the peripatetic pieces together. A vast pile emerged that looked ominously like a tax return in the middle of a nervous breakdown. Where to begin?

Having only made a list of scenes and written a brief outline, I began to wonder if I ought to phone Hilary, reimburse her for lunch and call it quits *now*. Rifling around, though, I realized that a huge amount of it was already written, albeit in short, unconnected scenes. I bunged on a CD of seventies music and set about numbering the chaotic postcards, notes and everything else.

The thought that 'someone really ought to write a book about this place' had refrained throughout my childhood. I remember a sense from everyone who lived through this last gasp of Empire that it was worthy of being recorded in some way. The cast list was composed of expats who had left England young, or scarpered out of India in 1947, dribbled down through colonial Africa, from Kenya, via Nyasaland, Northern Rhodesia, Bechuanaland and Basutoland, and finally fetched up in Swaziland, the last outpost of the Union Jack on the continent. There was a braying chorus of 'We're going home' on one hand, and 'England's gone to the dogs' on the other. Most faced the dilemma of either trying to hold on to a colonial standard of living and sense of self-importance that had a fast-approaching sell-by date, or sailing back to a life of anonymity in a semi in Datchet, or Norwich, or wherever.

The circumstances of my parents' pain-filled divorce were so riddled with rumour, recrimination and misunderstandings that, in writing about it, I hoped somehow to make sense of it all and expose the hypocrisy of the colonial hoi polloi sitting in judgement. Secrets are like poison and I wanted to burst the pustule. At the same time, I wanted to revisit and recreate the sheer malarkey and joy of being an adolescent amongst adults revving up for an amateur production of *Camelot*.

Hilary calls. 'Can you come in and pitch to the finance team at Blackjack Productions in Soho Square tomorrow?'

The next day I put on my confidence pants, go to Soho Square and hit the button for the seventh floor. In the boardroom I plonk down, riddled with doubt that my story's too fragile to hold their attention. I breathe deeply and smile as they enter.

No going back. The pitch is not a million miles away from the one I gave in Robert Altman's *The Player*.

When I hear the words 'an intimate epic' spurt from my maw, I realize just how beyond myself I have actually got. All the more so when I quote scenes and examples from the masterworks of Messrs Kubrick, Coppola and Altman along the way. Smokescreens and mirrors.

So far they are all giving me the hugest benefit of my doubts and continue nodding and smiling, even laughing at the *Camelot* shenanigans.

'How soon can we see a draft?' And with a do-re-mi agents are negotiating a writing-directing fee. The 'pitch' is now a 'proposition'.

## October to November 1999

Bruce Robinson, who wrote and directed *Withnail and I*, advised me to start my screenplay with the tried and tested precept of thinking about what happened on the day it begins that had never happened before. My beginning is inadvertently witnessing my mother's adultery on the front seat of the car whilst I 'slept' in the back. The middle: my father's drunken attempt to blow my brains out one night when I emptied a case of his whisky. And an ending: my father's bizarre funeral when a young Swazi priest attempted to raise him from the dead. I decided on these three foundation posts, then set about filling in the gaps – which plunged me into examining my past and the people I knew with urgent ferocity. Firstly I made a long list of key events, characters, incidents and anecdotes to try and find a narrative thread to bind them all together.

One of my earliest images of growing up in sixties Swaziland was the contrast between the black Swazis, kitted out in traditional Mahiya national dress, which kept them cool and casual-looking, and the pasty Brits, who wore clothes that never seemed to suit the hot weather. Those that did brave the sun soon burnt to an angry red crisp like a bursting sausage. There was a brigade of horsy women with enormous arses, moustaches and jolly-hockey-sticks ideas about everything walloping about in all directions, whose skins had weathered like leather and whose breath and hands always smelled of horse saliva and dung. The men all seemed to be obsessed with their balls – big ones, small ones, red ones, white or black ones. Any and *every* sport featuring balls seemed to be an obsession. Given the heat, no television, nine-to-five working hours, cheap servants and lots of leisure time, it was entertainment.

If known familiarly, all adults had to be addressed with the prefix Uncle or Aunty, though they were not blood relations. Unless you were American. There were American kids who even called their parents by their Christian names, which was considered really outré. People generally scoffed and laughed at them behind their backs for being 'different', but the fact remained that they landed on the moon first. The largest American presence was the Peace Corps hippies – or Vietnam draft dodgers, depending on which side of the political fence you sat. They were the third 'tribe', sandal-wearing, bearded and bead-bedecked folk who bridged the visual gap between the milk-bottle Brits and coffee-brown Swazis.

My story always seems to start with a betrayal. The image of my mother in a paisley flared pantsuit swaying wantonly to 'Winchester Cathedral' with eyes clamped shut is something that I watched with the secret knowledge of having witnessed her carrying on with a man who wasn't my father in the front seat of his car, whilst I was supposedly asleep in the back.

Seeing what I should never have seen. Feeling guilt for being a witness. It is the precise moment when my childhood ended and my 'divided' view of the world began – at once both a participant in and observer of my own life. I am grateful in retrospect that it has proved to be such a creative, if sometimes painful, force ever since.

It was the moment I started keeping a secret diary. It was also the moment I gave up on God. Although I kept praying in the weeks that followed my mother's dawn departure that God might intervene on my behalf, when she clearly wasn't coming back I gave up on him. Seeing my father begging and weeping when I was ten years old, and not succeeding in bringing her back, was a big unspoken realization. When you see that the very man who is supposed to be strong and in control is not, and whom, as a child, you naturally invest with superhuman powers that it turns out he doesn't have, then your faith in the old order gets shot to pieces.

When he got paralytically drunk and fell asleep in his chair, I childishly accepted that although he was in agony, we'd be all right, just so long as nobody else ever found out! Watching *The Sound of Music*, which finally made it to Swaziland four years after it was made, I willed Julie Andrews to leap off the Alps and come and save us. The schism between the face shown and not shown, the nature of pretence and self-image, is what really interests me.

It takes me a couple of months to complete a first draft which clocks in at 140 pages – too long, according to the time-honoured screen ratio of one page to a minute of screen time. I edit it down to 115 pages and nervously post it off to Hilary in Barbados.

She is enthusiastic, has very few script suggestions and is gung-ho about setting up a casting director and getting it up and running immediately. Mary Selway, who cast me in my first film, agrees to do the casting and without so much as a do-re-mi, Hilary organizes a location recce trip to Swaziland, where we meet the King and are granted permission by him to film out there. Everything seems to be going smoothly and quickly, and various actors' names are bandied back and forth for the main roles. Hilary is convinced it will be a snap to get actors interested and attached. Her positive enthusings lull me into thinking that I won't have to do multiple rewrites of the script, as is customary, and that we can realistically aim to get it cast and therefore financed before the year is out. Securing 'names' for the lead roles in turn attracts finance. The chicken-and-egg syndrome – actors and agents want to know if the film is fully financed, and financiers want to know which famous actors are on board.

The first warning signal comes from Mary Selway, who opines that the script is not yet ready to be sent out to actors and that it would be improved by focusing more on the inner workings of the family in the story. Reality check.

Mary reluctantly withdraws a week later due to the recurrence of her cancer. The casting director Celestia Fox generously agrees to take over, and she has valuable suggestions to cut down some of the peripheral Peace Corps characters and to focus on the father–son relationship. The story covers about four years, and she is very insistent that we try and cast a single actor to play the lead boy, rather than attempt to find an eleven-year-old and a fifteen-year-old who can morph into each other.

Eric Felner at Working Title rejects the script in its present form, expressing doubt about the *Camelot* amateur-dramatic section of the story. An agent says that as all the characters are so thoroughly unpleasant, she is disinclined to send it to any of her clients for consideration.

Minnie Driver turns it down.

Brenda Blethyn and Anna Chancellor 'pass'.

Major wake-up call. I feel foolish for having willingly believed the script was ready to send out so soon. Portcullis down and drawbridge up. Rewrite. Rewrite. Rewrite.

Harry Hook, writer-director and a very good friend, helpfully puts me in touch with Philip Palmer, a script editor who kindly agrees to give me his professional opinion which I pay him for.

Philip's opening paragraph goes like this: 'This is a beautifully observed, delightfully written script. I love all the droll asides in the scene directions. Like all the mad incidents that are so unlikely – the African evangelical priest who jumps on Harry's coffin and tries to bring the corpse back to life – they must be true. The script succeeds totally in conjuring up the bizarre, claustrophobic, eccentric, hermetically sealed expat universe, and takes us on a tour of that world.'

So far so good, but the next four pages are a detailed breakdown of everything that is 'wrong' with it. Deep-breath time, and I sort out just how much I agree with him or not. Significantly, Philip reiterates notes I have had from elsewhere – that the film is 'first and foremost the story about a father and son relationship. This *is* the story. Excise material that does not in some way reflect on the underlying character story about a father and son.'

As I'm anxious to try and get it as right as possible in order not to blow my chances before I've even properly begun, I request that Hilary give me some time to act upon Philip's suggestions before sending the revised script out to anyone else.

### October to December 2000

Whilst shooting a children's film in Australia, I do yet another rewrite. During my time there, I pursue Toni Colette as a possibility for the key character of the American stepmother, Ruby. Toni *could* play it Australian rather than American, thus maintaining the character's essential 'outsider' status.

### 15 January 2001

Hilary has worked with director Mike Newell, who generously agrees to read the script and give me two hours of notes. He focuses on the divide between what goes on behind the central family's closed doors and the strict social hierarchy of the colonial society. He manages to be ruthlessly incisive, encouraging, charming and friendly all at once, and I'm very grateful.

I reread William Golding's pithy experiences of being a screenwriter, in which he underlines that *everyone* has a different opinion and inevitably describes the kind of film *they* would like to see from your script. As helpful and hugely informing as the notes, feedback, advice and opinions are, you have to decide on your own which direction to go in. There's nothing so easy as advising what should be cut or included, and nothing so hard as implementing these apparently simple suggestions. The moment one scene is cut, it has a knock-on effect that impacts elsewhere.

The likelihood of it ever reaching a screen seems utterly remote at this moment. I call Bruce Robinson, who reassures me with, 'Welcome to rewrite hell.'

Rewrite. Groundhog day. Dog-day afternoons. Call it what you will, but as soon as you think you've got your dish ready to serve, it spaghettis all over the place and you have to clean up the mess. There's a Charlie Brown 'Arrgh' in a bubble over my head.

Rupert Everett, whom I know from Robert Altman's *Prêt-à-Porter*, is a lifelong friend of Celestia Fox and a client of Duncan Heath, Hilary's ex-husband who owns the ICM actors' agency in London. Both Celestia and Duncan are keen that Rupert play the lead role of my father, even though he has relatively recently 'come out' in *My Best Friend's Wedding*. Although I'm assured he will hugely help raise the finance, I'm not convinced he'd be right for the part, but send it off to him. He says he is 'interested, with reservations'. Ditto.

He also knows Toni Collette, whom I have now spent three months pursuing via her agent. The delay is due to her doing films back to back. I hope she reads it soon.

### 2 February 2001

A 'Dear Richard' email from Toni's agent:

I have spoken with Toni and unfortunately she feels *Wah-Wah* is not a project for her. Thank you for your patience and I apologise for any delay in response.

I feel lumbar-punctured by this and am unable to rewrite all day. Celestia and I bandy actor names about, and as with Mary Selway, *everything* is very personal – who you rate or don't, who is a reputed nightmare to work with, who is likely even to consider a no-budget first-time-writer-director's project, shooting in a southern corner of Africa. I need to pull myself up by the proverbials and have courage.

Back to the old drawing board, and the schizoid nature of it whereby you invest thought and passion into why and how this or that actor is perfect for the part, and are then forced to forsake and forget them when they turn you down. Even though I know it is in the nature of this circus, it's a bollock-kicker the day you get the news. If rejection is part and parcel of *every* actor's life experience, it pales significantly compared to the turn-downs already encountered *trying* to get this film off the ground.

But then, nobody is exactly forcing me to pursue this dream.

### 1 March 2001

Blizzards, train crashes, foot-and-mouth disease, transport at a standstill and a general air of everything falling apart. The threatened American actors' strike in June means that no American actors could work until it's resolved, and as we are faintly hoping to shoot in August and September, the dry winter season, we'll have to pursue non-Americans.

Rachel Griffiths is our next choice, but she has recently had breakaway success in *Six Feet Under*, so I know this is pipe-dreaming. We try anyway. Everything takes much longer than my genetic short-fuse attention span is used to.

# DEVELOPMENT

## 6 March 2001

Finally completed another draft after making a mountain of notes, and feel euphoric. For twenty-four hours.

This was followed by the sense that nothing fundamental has yet been achieved, although I'm aware this might be the norm in this process. I persevere every day, one day at a time like a recovering junkie, *willing* the film to happen, somehow.

The new version is winging its way to Rachel Griffiths in Australia.

I receive an email from Glenda Stephens in Swaziland, whom I have known since the year dot, who reports that her mother-in-law, Coral, has just celebrated her ninety-first birthday and her father-in-law, Bob, has just turned ninety-six. She plans to take them on holiday whilst we are filming at their home, Boshimela (which means 'the house with many chimneys'), in Pigg's Peak in the north of Swaziland.

I'm invited to a dinner at Blenheim Palace hosted by Lady Spencer-Churchill, and meet Michael Jackson. I'm seated opposite a man with the saddest, loneliest eyes I've ever seen. It's bizarre to hear him speak in the quavering voice of a five-year-old girl. He was on the brink of tears throughout, barely ate a mouthful and got emotional for no discernible reason. Absolutely riveting to witness, yet gruesomely uncomfortable. It's like talking to someone who has lost a layer of skin and has no defences. He talked about the importance of parents reading stories to their children at bedtime. His corpse-white skin, red-lipsticked mouth, pencil-slim nose and what appears to be the gauze of his wig clearly visible on his forehead where the glue hasn't adhered properly are *utterly* bizarre.

### 7 March 2001

Mailed script to Julie Walters for the supporting role of Gwen Traherne, whose husband John has run off with Lauren – my mother. I
worked with her years ago on an ill-fated but hugely enjoyable film
to make, *Killing Dad*. Always a slight quandary sending the script to
someone you know, shifting things onto a professional footing –
potentially making a turn-down less easy to do if you know each
other. She has just been nominated for her second Oscar for her
stunning performance in *Billy Elliot*, so the chances are she will be
booked into the next millennium.

### 8 March 2001

Julie Walters calls me in the evening and says the magic word, 'YES!'
She loves the script, and while she knows it is a supporting role, and
we will film in Africa, she is so enthused and passionate about it that
she instantly restores my flagging faith. The moment I put the phone
down, I jumped up and down like a kangaroo on Ecstasy.

### 20 March 2001

Rachel Griffiths has 'passed' – she 'needs a holiday and not keen to
go to Africa for five weeks'.

At least she has responded quickly. I guess this yo-yoing is par for
the course, even if there are more ons and offs than Zsa Zsa Gabor's
girdle.

# DEVELOPMENT

Just seen Christopher Guest's hilarious mockumentary *Best in Show* and Catherine O'Hara is a real potential Ruby, if a little mature. It depends on who we get to play Harry, the male lead – my father. She is also Canadian, which might theoretically exempt her if the actors' strike goes ahead. I track down her agent and post the script.

## 21 March 2001

I've been cast as a footman in Robert Altman's *Gosford Park*, playing the sidekick to Alan Bates. It's an upstairs-downstairs murder mystery with an epic cast list. This is the third time I have worked for Altman, a *real* pleasure and I'm thrilled to be included, even if it requires short back and sides, stiff collars and waitering all day, with the odd stolen clutch at a passing serving maid's arse as distraction. Altman's magician's skills at making everyone feel valued and included make for a very collaborative and pleasurable working atmosphere. He rightly anticipates that all egos are best kept in check by a simple self-policing process amongst the cast list, which includes Dame Eileen Atkins, Sir Alan Bates, Bob Balaban, Charles Dance, Stephen Fry, Sir Michael Gambon, Tom Hollander, Sir Derek Jacobi, Dame Helen Mirren, Kelly Macdonald, Jeremy Northam, Clive Owen, Ryan Phillippe, Kristin Scott Thomas, Dame Maggie Smith, James Wilby and Emily Watson.

I'm awestruck by Altman's power to attract such a list, so grateful to be in such illustrious company *and* have a job that will offer a distraction from my rewrites and casting problems.

## 17 April 2001

The complete arc of an actor's life is on offer, ranging from the scrub-faced, keen-eyed wonderment visible in the eyes of the fledglings fresh from drama school, some of whose chewn fingernails belie their outward swagger and 'cool', onwards and upwards through a Hind's variety of neurotics and the upwardly mobilized.

Laurence Fox, the young lanky son of James Fox, is wondering out loud how to cope with the publicity he has to do for his first film, *The Hole*, opposite Thora Birch.

Another young blade, in his final fortnight at RADA, is gob-smacked to have secured an agent *and* a role in his first film – an Altman film at that – that will catapult him to instant stardom. He hopes.

Up the ladder a little, the 'totty' department of beautiful twenty-somethings, with all their charms and looks intact, are blooming and buoyant with flirt and possibility. Knowing the national predilection for favouring unsightly old bangers as opposed to flawless-skinned young fillies, their sell-by dates might well arrive all too soon. Unless an enterprising American director saves them from the sitcom trough.

A Lautrec-sized actor is already obsessing about not having another job to go to after this wraps, despite the fact that we are only halfway through. He does the lunchtime round-up of who is doing what next, frantically calling his agent on his mobile bemoaning the fact that he doesn't have another gig to go to yet. He looks hugely relieved when I tell him that I'm not booked yet either.

A pair of males in their late thirties are testing each other's antlers, especially as one of them is no longer making as many films as he'd like to and cannot comprehend why this fellow stag is hoovering up every film in sight and never stops working. It's the fatal 'Shall I compare my career to the summer's day of yours?' syndrome. Most often there simply is no logic to how this stuff happens – as I know all too acutely, having despaired of ever being employed again, sitting through the waking nightmare of the *Hudson Hawk* premiere a decade ago. Despite the turkey-sized sizzler we were about to suffer, I was saved by a tap on the shoulder from Robert Altman and Tim Robbins, sitting behind me, who offered me a role in *The Player*.

Kristin Scott Thomas, just forty-ish and fresh from a duo of films opposite Robert Redford and Harrison Ford, is coolly assessing the salary *shift* from a Hollywood studio salary to the scrimp indie budget of an Altman ensemble film where there are two salary tiers, neither of which you'd land a mortgage with. She wonders out loud about the point of spending the rest of her life dressing up and pretending.

Bob Balaban is one of our producers and fellow actors – a Zelig of a man who seems to know everyone and has been in everything from *Friends* to Woody Allens, Altmans, Christopher Guests and mainstream flicks. Hugely likeable, he is happy to pop up in films all over the place.

Ryan Phillippe – twenty-six and married to Reese Witherspoon – is the only other American actor. He is known amongst us from the teen remake of *Dangerous Liaisons*, is very serious about his work and is in Cruise-control of imminent stardom – or so it seems, such is his innate confidence compared to his English contemporaries. He has replaced Jude Law, who had to withdraw at the eleventh hour.

Emily Watson, despite two Oscar nominations, is as open and warm-hearted as you'd hope her to be, without any la-di-dah or career embitterment, her huge Bambi eyes as wide as a five-year-old's at the opportunity to board the Altman carousel. Charles Dance says he hasn't worked for eighteen months, which really takes me aback. And doubtless reassures Mr Lautrec that he is not alone.

Sir Michael Gambon is an outrageously funny storyteller and purveyor of filthy anecdotes who verbally mines an ironic seam, claiming he lives off the crusts and crumbs of the likes of Sir Anthony Hopkins, which none of us believe for a minute, but he is very entertaining at it.

Alan Bates, now sixty-seven, has been Oscar-nominated, bemedalled, won shelf-loads of awards, as have his peers Dame Maggie Smith and Dame Eileen Atkins. He is an unstoppably funny font of stories about past triumphs and flops, and still hungry for it all.

Then there's Bob Altman, our captain and commander, at seventy-six as energetic and passionate about making films against all studio odds as he ever was, haranguing the corporate politics and executive-crammed nature of mainstream Hollywood with the seasoned gall of a veteran gladiator. He flirts and seduces everyone up, down and sideways.

I search for a common denominator and settle on a quote from American choreographer Martha Graham, who identified that the 'creative artist lives in a state of divine discontent'.

Funny and desperate by turns, there is nothing like listening to an earful of actors worrying 'Should I or shouldn't I do *this* job or *that*, and what about my reputation?' and suchlike bollocks, then have it all undercut by overhearing a unit driver ask, 'So who's that geezer over there, then?' and listen to some poor bastard trying to explain to his blank-faced mate that he is a knight of the theatrical realm. If the cast had to line up on nearby Hendon High Street, how many of the illustrious faces would be recognized?

The late Roddy McDowell asked me how I saw my old age, to which I looked back blankly. He said, 'You have two choices – either follow the path of ninety-nine per cent of our profession and become bitter and twisted as the roles and monies diminish, *or* embrace it all and thank your lucky stars for the great ride you're having. Ups and downs included. It's your choice.' Sobering and wise.

# DEVELOPMENT

## *4 May 2001*

My agent emails one of those ubiquitous mini-interview question-naires that do the rounds of every other actor:

1. **What's the best thing about being British?**
   *Bollshy, ballsy, busty, Branston pickly, bulldoggedly beautiful.*
2. **Childhood seaside holiday in full?**
   *Soggy sandwiches, sandy sleeping bags, sodden skies and sadistic winds.*
3. **Favourite British pastimes?**
   *Grumbling, laughing, moaning, grizzling, giggling, groaning, gagging, then watching EastEnders and feeling a whole lot better than anyone else does on Albert Square.*
4. **Who defines Britishness for you?**
   *Basil and Sybil Fawlty.*
5. **What song should be the National Anthem?**
   *'All Things Bright and Beautiful'.*
6. **When was the last time you felt proud to be British?**
   *Every time any big shot makes a toss box of himself, giving the rest of us a good laugh.*
7. **What are you up to at the moment?**
   *Filming Robert Altman's Gosford Park.*

## *15 May 2001*

All the upstairs 'toffs' have departed, as has the whole unit from Wrotham Park, to Shepperton Studios where production designer

Stephen Altman has immaculately recreated an entire downstairs set of bedrooms, corridors and kitchens. There is a huge visual contrast between the upstairs world of languid-bodied, perfectly powdered beauties called Camilla, Kristin, Claudia and Natasha, and the downstairs staff, most of whom have been cast for their ability to portray battleship boilers with names like Tilly, Meg, Laura and Tessie.

A steady stream of visitors come to pay their professional respects to Bob, who seems to thrive best when surrounded by huge numbers of people, all of whom enjoy his innate sociability and contagious delight. It is the most relaxed and enjoyable set I have ever worked on, and the usual hours of waiting around between lighting and technical set-ups are barely noticeable as there is always so much going on at once and so many people to talk to. Stories, stories, stories. And then more of them.

### 22 May 2001

I've known Sir Elton John and David Furnish for some years and, with their encouragement, I'd sent my script to their Rocket Pictures company. Again there was that dread sense of crossing friendship/ professional fences, and I experienced an instant flush of embarrassment and regret at ever having done so when David's very polite letter arrives:

> The problem with pursuing material like *Wah-Wah* is that it is more of a 'small' story. This type of British film has become virtually impossible to finance these days. After dedicating three years to producing *Women Talking Dirty*, we have decided to focus the company's energies on bigger, higher-concept films and have two animated films in the pipeline with Disney. As a result I'm afraid we will have to pass on *Wah-Wah*.

## *25 May 2001*

Final day on *Gosford Park*. My last line – 'Her ladyship is about to leave, miss' – echoes the *first* line I ever had in a play at drama school. Having gone full circle, I wonder if this will be the last sentence I utter for money this year.

The American writers' strike is off; hoping the actors' strike goes the same way. I'm often asked what working for Robert Altman is like and this is the answer: having visited his unique planet a couple of times previously on *The Player* and *Prêt-à-Porter*, in Los Angeles and Paris respectively, and now London for *Gosford Park*, geography has nothing much to do with the 'landscape' – in Altman-land, you require no passport, visa or special travel requirements other than your talent and a total willingness to abandon yourself to Altmania.

You work for kibbutz-ish wages and none of the usual megastars-in-trailers and cameo-actors-in-cubbyholes usuals. Everyone is democratically ruled by this benign, omnipotent Wizard of Oz. Altman grew up in Kansas City and for the past forty years stars have been dancing down his yellow-brick road with legendary regularity. Unlike the wizard of fiction, he does not frighten with smoke, thunder and mirrors, but rather draws back the curtain and invites everyone in.

On any given day the entire cast might be called in, and instead of them grumbling about the lack of lines or Jacuzzis, he creates an atmosphere akin to a house party amongst good friends.

By using multiple cameras, nobody much knows if they are the centre of attention at any given moment, which means that every actor is wholly consumed by their character and agenda at all times. No matter where you choose to look, or however many characters are vying for attention, it's clear what everyone is doing. Added to which, after lunch *everyone* is invited to watch the previous day's rushes – usually the prerogative of the director and inner circle. Altman makes it a social event that invisibly glues everyone to the project, and affords the opportunity to see everyone else's work before it has been edited. It's such a logical and simple idea you'd think that everyone would make films this way. He is unique in my experience.

He is also as curious about what is going on in the corner of the room as he is in the centre-stage activities – hence the signature large-cast, community-style stories of *Nashville*, *MASH*, *A Wedding*, *Short Cuts* and so on.

The Hollywood penchant for good guy/bad guy and babes either running towards or away from a series of spectacular explosions is Planet Anathema to his sensibilities. His entire interest and focus is in the minutiae of human behaviour.

If you ask him for direction he will say, 'I haven't a clue what to tell you – surprise me. Show me something I've never seen before.' Like the perfect ringmaster, he sets up a scene, switches on the lights, strikes up the band and hollers, *'Action!'* and the circus of humanity gets up on its hind legs and performs a perfectly synchronized display of Life in all its variations, including Love and of course the seven deadly sins.

Whether critically lauded or damned, the actual experience of entering Altman-land is always the same – an irresistible cocktail of comedy, gossip, intrigue and star-gazing. What more could a boy from Swazi want?

### *June 2001 to March 2002*

Hilary Heath, my producer, drops a bombshell – she is withdrawing to pursue an alternative career as a drug-rehab counsellor in Barbados. But not before a last-minute attempt to interest Hugh Grant in the lead, as she produced one of his earlier films. Unsurprisingly, he passes.

She sets me up with Little Bird Films, who agree to act as executive producers. I can't help but feel somewhat marooned. Catherine O'Hara politely 'passes' on the 'project'. What euphemisms are there at this point for 'up shite creek without a paddle'?

The script is sent to Colin Firth for the lead role. He too politely passes four months later. The list of financeable British actors in this age range is very short. Having re-jigged my brain as to what each actor might bring to the role of my father, the offer goes out to Ralph Fiennes in late October. However, he is in preparation for shooting *Red Dragon* and his agent warns me that Ralph doesn't read scripts whilst doing a role, so we'll have to be patient.

I rewrite, rewrite and rewrite again, reconfigure and attempt to second-guess what might or might not happen next. It's like trying to juggle with jelly. Will it or won't it ever happen, that is the never-answered, never-ending question . . .

The Twin Towers are bombed in New York, and with the world gone suddenly upside down, my worries about getting a movie off the ground seem irrelevant.

Do-re-mi and months dwindle away, prompting me to accept playing the villain in a *Hound of the Baskervilles* adaptation for the BBC on the Isle of Man in April.

### 30 April 2002

Email from the ever-loyal Celestia Fox reporting on the Fiennes situation:

*Red Dragon* has gone over schedule, so Ralph is finishing on that as well as shooting *Maid in Manhattan* till end of July, thereafter will do *Girl with a Pearl Earring* – if it goes – then starts rehearsing *Brand* for the RSC in October. Your best chance is if *Pearl* doesn't go and he is free in August–September. Will know next week.

So with his dance card full, his likelihood is highly *unlikely*, especially as he has not actually committed to mine in the first place! But hang in there.

## *May to July 2002*

I'm cast to play Sir Hudson Lowe in *Monsieur N.*, a French film about Napoleon's last year on St Helena. Lowe was the English governor suspected of poisoning the little chap. The film is directed by Antoine de Caunes, shooting in and around Cape Town and Paris. It's a welcome distraction from the nothing-happening-hurry-up-and-wait syndrome.

The French team are one hundred per cent behind the director, it's generously scheduled and seemingly without any executive interference. The producer Marie-Castille Mention-Schaar is very low key and calm. The shoot is hugely enjoyable, despite the nerves from having to do some scenes in French. The producer is keen that I send her my script, but I agree to do so only after we have wrapped.

When she and her producing partner Pierre Kubel read it, they call the following morning and ask if they can do a co-production with Little Bird Films. I'm *thrilled* by this prompt response. We set up a meeting to take place after I see Ralph, who has relayed word that he is 'very interested' and asks if we can have lunch when he gets back, on 15 October.

## 15 October 2002

Meet Ralph for lunch at a restaurant near his home in Hammersmith, and show him the eighteen-minute Handycam film I have made of all the Swazi locations in story order with basic sound effects and music to give him an idea of where I am 'going'. We worked together briefly in the last century on a charity performance of *Bent* (with Ian McKellen and the late great Ian Charleson), before he became a film star. He is as enthusiastic about the script as I could wish for, and at the end of a very good meeting asks if he could have another couple of weeks to make his final decision. If I had a tail, it would be wagging like a well-fed, pampered puppy's.

The 4 p.m. meeting with Little Bird Films and Loma Nasha Productions from Paris is a disaster. The Little Bird producer is delayed in Glasgow and phones to say he won't get there until 6 p.m. Then he is delayed further and sends his associate along instead, who has not read the script, knows precious little about the whole project and basically tells the French pair that there is scant precedent for successful co-production between England and France, which goes down like a bucket of.

As a result, Marie-Castille and Pierre Kubel ask if they can take over the film as they feel sure they can raise all the money themselves. Their passion for the script and front-footed attitude convinces me that this is the right way to go.

The contract I had with Hilary Heath stipulated that the rights to my script automatically revert to me in March 2003. As there is no possibility of the film being financed and set up before then, I politely withdraw from Little Bird on these grounds. I hope that this decision will *finally* get the film on its way to shoot mid-2003.

### 17 December 2002

I receive a glowing email from Marie-Castille saying that the French camera crew from *Monsieur N.* 'would love to shoot my film. Any news from Fiennes?'

Ralph came to our Christmas party and said he couldn't stop thinking about the script and location promo, which is a good sign, and to please have further patience given that he is really keen but cannot yet commit until he has opened his play in the New Year. He was as friendly and enthusiastic as I could hope for and I am prepared to wait for what might well be the longest casting seduction on record.

The prospect of the film really happening in the New Year seems suddenly feasible and a great Christmas present to end a year of stops and starts.

### 10 January 2003

The South African coordinator emails a barrage of detailed queries about precise locations, local contacts in Swaziland and the preliminary budgets prepared after my previous location recces with Hilary Heath. I am also asked about any insight or advice I might have about the country – to which I reply that I still know a fair number of people there, but as no one has ever made a film in Swaziland before, there is no infrastructure or anyone with filming experience. The advantage, though, is that there is enormous goodwill and curiosity, and all the locations are within easy reach of one another. A doctor friend has advised that the population is approximately forty per cent HIV-positive, which the crew will have to be warned about. 'Tomorrow is another day' is my experience, and nothing happens instantly, so it's vital to be aware that pre-production will have to be very methodical, especially with regard to securing work permits for everyone. Everything requires negotiation, patience and incredible politeness, as opposed to barnstorming aggression and demands. As with everywhere else, who you know counts for a great deal and the meeting with the King instantly opened doors. However, three years have passed since our meeting and we cannot blithely rely on that goodwill lasting.

However, just being asked these kinds of questions provokes my nostrils to scent *action*. Ralph Fiennes is free in September–October, so *hoping* he comes through.

### 15 January 2003

I had asked cinematographer Andrew Dunn to do the film and he has agreed, dates pending. However, with the French co-production points system, there is pressure to have as many key French technicians on board as possible. Andrew is free in September and Marie-Castille says she is willing to employ him, but that all post-production will have to be done in France as the film is being shot entirely in Africa.

### 16 January 2003

I get a kind letter from David Thompson at BBC Films saying that they have too many African projects on the go already and cannot come on board. He says he was a young VSO volunteer in Swaziland and attended the Independence ceremony in 1968. His ameliorating tone makes the rejection letter easier to take on board.

## 1 March 2003

Coral Stephens has died at the age of ninety-three in Pigg's Peak, ending a whole chapter, verse and history of colonial Swaziland. She started up a traditional loom-weaving cottage industry using mohair, cotton, wool and vegetable dyes, which mushroomed into a mini-global production line. I'm unsure what will happen to the Boshimela house and whether we will still be able to rent it as the main location or not.

Andrew Dunn calls to let me know that he is booked to do two films between now and the autumn, but will keep me posted. The juggling act of trying to keep the phantom ship of this film afloat is increasingly smoke and mirrors. That is, theoretically, until Ralph Fiennes makes his decision. I'm trying hard to avoid talking as if I have swallowed the Domesday Book when folk ask, 'So when does your film start?'

## 25 March 2003

Celestia Fox puts in a call to Ralph's agent, who informs her that he will not make a decision until his play opens on 19 April. This is now driving me completely crazy.

## 28 April 2003

Saw Kristin Scott Thomas, who casually let drop the news that Ralph Fiennes is doing his sister Martha's next film in his September break.

My guts plunged, and I immediately called ICM to check if her film was financed and definitely going or not. Unsure. But it now seems pretty clear he is *not* going to commit to mine. Write a Custer's last stand email to Ralph asking if he can make a decision either way as Cannes is around the corner and the producers are keen to announce the film and principal casting.

### 5 May 2003

My agent relays the news that Ralph has 'passed' on the film. Today is my forty-sixth birthday and this is not the present I wanted to get. It has, however, ended the farce of the endless wait.

Called agent Tor Belfrage on the *slightest* off-chance that her client Daniel Day-Lewis might have changed his mind and started considering doing films again. The answer is no. I feel I've finally exhausted the list of British actors in the forty-to-fifty age range who would be right for the part and are a 'name'. At this point I am willing to have Mickey Rooney play my father!

Though casting an older actor will have an impact on whoever else is cast, I reconsider. The older group includes Jeremy Irons.

### 20 May 2003

Jeremy Irons turns it down on the grounds that the role is too unsympathetic. The fact that he won his Oscar for essaying Claus von Bülow tickertapes across my cranium.

### 29 May 2003

Celestia calls to say that Rupert Everett has reconsidered and is now keen to do the film. *Real* quandary for me. He is incredibly funny, charming and the best of company; however, he is the only actor I can think of who has ever 'come out' at the zenith of his career and in the role of my twice-married heterosexual father-with-son, will potentially create problems of credibility. Email Steve Martin for his advice. He says to go with Rupert – Hollywood has a very short memory.

### 2 June 2003

Lunch in Soho with Rupert, who is as wickedly funny and irreverent as ever and on top form. We talk about the script in more detail and I still get the sense that he is forever going to vacillate, as happened over two years ago when we met. However, we shake hands and I leave with his tacit acceptance of the role. At 4 p.m., I speak to our mutual agency ICM and hear that Rupert is about to be offered a role in a film written and debut-directed by Julian Fellowes, opposite Emily Watson and Tom Wilkinson, shooting in September, fully financed and ready to go.

As we have *no* finance in place whatsoever, there is no chance of keeping Rupert and wouldn't dream of doing so on the off-chance that we get money in time.

Leave a jokey message on his answer machine saying that I know about his offer and decision and only to call me back if he is *not* going to do the film.

Having endured fourteen months waiting on Ralph Fiennes, it's been cartoon-fast securing an actor at 2 p.m., only to find him lost again at 4 p.m.

No chance the film can go this year. Marie-Castille suggests Gabriel Byrne to play Harry. Genius idea and I kick myself for not thinking of him before. Send him the script.

### 5 June 2003

Agree to play the lead in *The Story of an African Farm*, filming in the Karoo desert three hours out of Cape Town. I play a conman who adopts an Irish accent to try and fleece a woman out of her farm and fortune, set in the 1870s. Shooting starts on 8 September through October.

### 13 June 2003

Message from Gabriel Byrne's agent Teri Hayden in Dublin asking for dates and whether the film is fully financed, and most thrillingly saying that Gabriel really likes the script. I could almost get superstitious on this Friday the 13th hearing this sliver of hope.

### 23 June 2003

Waaaaaah-Waaaaaah!! Gabriel Byrne *wants* to do the film. I levitated and swivelled and felt as if my head might actually do a Linda Blair 360-degree *Exorcist*-style turn. Yippity-doo-dah and Yi-haaaaaaaaa ululate from my throat and very hot tears spurt down my face. The relief, the relief, the *relief*. After *so* long. Even if he has a caveat to accommodate some script changes and adjustments, right now I am ready to rewrite the Magna Carta for him.

Meet the man himself at the Charlotte Street Hotel in Soho for lunch, and his charm is all-pervasive from the moment we meet, in his way of speaking to the waitress and anyone else who comes his way. His passion for the script and identification are at such a profound level that I am frankly astonished. He speaks non-stop and with such poetic eloquence that a great deal of time passes very swiftly. Philosophical. Curious. Sympathetic. Handsome and soulful. Sounds like a dating-agency shortlist, but he is all of these things. He watches the short location film that I made and is all the more enthralled and committed to the film. We talk about casting, his script readjustments and some worries about the character not being sympathetic enough, but *everything* about Gabriel, like my father, is innately charming, loveable and sympathetic. I take on board his concerns and promise to take another pass at the script trying to incorporate his suggestions.

To actually be talking about the script in this kind of depth, rather than expending so much time and energy trying to get the script to agents and *read* by their clients, is a bloody marvel and reminds me that *this* is the reason and motor for it all. Having felt like the poor sod that never got a date, left isolated on the ever-widening shelf of oblivion, I feel like I've ended up with the prom queen, head girl, Miss World, number one 'totty' of them all today.

I'm prompted to write a 'Dear Gabriel' email:

I could not be a happier man today if I tried. THANK YOU, THANK YOU, THANKYOU!!!

Any worries I have about him not sounding English enough are put on the back burner. I run around Richmond Park like Roadrunner, trying to believe we are now in with a chance to get going! *All* the agonies of the past two years dissolve momentarily away.

# DEVELOPMENT

## *26 June 2003*

Now to cast the character of Ruby. Having tried the American and Australians without success, my wife moots the idea of Juliette Binoche. Marie-Castille is not keen and suggests Emmanuelle Béart. It's a can of worms for me going the French route, as there are very few French actresses I can think of who speak English fluently enough for what I am after, and they tend to have an innate patina of sophistication and chic about them.

A French woman marrying into the hermetically sealed expat colonial community of Swaziland would require a rewrite and rethink, and Béart is not a natural comedian. However, I know that Marie-Castille will be assured of French financing having a French star to play the female lead. I email her saying that in all my years in Swaziland I only ever met one French woman, who was appalled by the food and lack of sophistication!

If Ruby is to have an innately vulgar warmth, Béart is nowhere near this.

Marie-Castille disagrees, claiming that she has seen her in a comedy 'in vulgar attitudes', which makes me laugh. The daft thing is that we have these casting conversations on the assumption that these stars will do the film, which considering that I have never written or directed one before, and Marie-Castille has only ever produced one – which flopped monumentally – we have no track record to speak of.

The sticky question of crew nationality comes up. I am told that I can have a British composer – Glaswegian Patrick Doyle, who has generously agreed to score it – and an English costume designer. Camera department, sound team and editor must be French to qualify as a co-production.

# THE WAH-WAH DIARIES

### *30 June 2003*

Meet Celestia Fox to start casting for boys and all the other supporting roles. Having secured Gabriel Byrne, Miranda Richardson (whom I had approached a year ago to play 'Lauren', which she accepted on the proviso that Mr Spielberg did not come up with a better offer at the same time) and Julie Walters, the pressure is now on to find a suitable Ruby.

Cate Blanchett, Renée Zellweger, Julianne Moore, Mira Sorvino, Sarah Jessica Parker, Mary Elizabeth Mastrantonio and Madeleine Stowe are all on my under-forty-five wish list. Along with every other wish list on the producing planet, no doubt. The over-forties list runs to Geena Davis and Meg Ryan, Catherine O'Hara having already 'passed' on the script.

The list for supporting roles (an oxymoron if ever there was one, given these names) is: Peter O'Toole, Dame Judi Dench, Albert Finney, Dame Eileen Atkins, Sir Alan Bates, Vanessa Redgrave, Charles Dance, Juliet Stephenson, Celia Imrie, Fenella Woolgar, Julian Wadham, Harriet Walters and Dame Diana Rigg. Well a man has to dream, right?

Celestia remains pretty adamant that we cast one boy to play the age range from eleven to fifteen, saying that it's extremely difficult to find two boys that match with such a small age gap, and you always risk losing an audience who identify with one actor and then have to re-adjust to a new one a third of the way in. *My* concern is that it will be very hard to find a boy who looks young and vulnerable enough to be asleep on the back seat of a car and to witness his mother's adultery, and then smoke his first joint and fall in love later in the story.

I watch every film I can starring age-changing actors to see how they have been done, from *My Left Foot* to *Young Winston* and anything else I can lay my hands on.

But, but, but – having *these* worries is small beer compared to the epic time it's taken to land the leading man!

Now aiming to shoot in spring 2004.

### 1 July 2003

Reality check: actor's fee information comes in, with Renée Zellweger costing $15 million for starters; Cate Blanchett is booked practically into the next millennium, and so forth. However, like moles, we blindly persevere and send scripts out in the hope of snagging some interest *anywhere*, now that we have three named cast members, a possible start date and the 'mirage' that we are financed. Even as I write down names and attach letters to the script for each actor via their agents, I know it is the equivalent of writing to the man in the moon. *Chasing the dream.*

### 9 July 2003

The first questions every American agent asks are: Is the film fully or partially financed? What is the budget and how much has been raised so far? I pass this hot potato directly over to Marie-Castille to deal with.

A touching email comes via my website from a Kenyan actor called Franky Mwangi saying he is 'a thirty-two-year-old Kenyan actor, but due to lack of growth hormones, I'm physically six to ten years old looking. I am in *Hidalgo* coming out in October playing the role of "slave boy" '. Reluctantly I have to write back that I am not casting an African 'child' of that age group, but hugely admire his chutzpah at finding out about the film and trying to get seen.

### 14 July 2003

'Dearest Richard' letter from Ralph Fiennes apologizing for taking so long to make his final decision owing to an incredible workload, expressing his admiration for the screenplay and his dilemma about choosing between my script and many others. Wishing me every success with *Wah-Wah*.

I am really grateful for his belated letter, but even more grateful that I am not reading it without having secured a leading actor in the meantime. Ralph is a true and very busy gentleman, deluged with offers, and I really appreciate his having taken the trouble to write to me.

### 18 July 2003

Just received confirmation from the King's adviser George Lys that there are plans to hold a joint Independence and thirty-fifth-birthday celebration for the King of Swaziland on 6 September at Somhlolo Stadium. I offer to pay for a skeletal camera and sound crew to take advantage of this opportunity and get footage of the massed Swazi warrior regiments for the Independence sequence in *Wah-Wah*.

### 20 July 2003

Grim email from Glenda Stephens about the Aids epidemic in Swaziland with huge numbers of orphaned children everywhere.

A nine-year-old boy is being sponsored to go to school, which is a two-hour walk away. Both parents died of Aids and when he gets home he has to get water, cook, sort out his younger sisters and tend to his demented grandmother. He's achieving nothing at school as he is too hungry and tired to do anything.

I feel guilty worrying about getting a film made on the one hand and trying to accommodate this terrible news on the other. What to do? Where to begin? An immediate thought is to have a charity premiere for the film specifically for orphaned children. Assuming the film ever gets made, that is.

Marie-Castille agrees to the Independence filming plan, hiring a camera and sound crew from South Africa. George Lys puts me in touch with Qhawe Mamba, who runs the outside-broadcast unit for Swazi TV, to help coordinate everything. Of huge help is the fact he will be filming the celebrations for local TV.

## *25 July 2003*

American agent:

> Meg Ryan is passing on *Wah-Wah*. Unfortunately it wasn't her cup of tea.

## *29 July 2003*

Christina Rice, whom I know through a mutual friend, is currently working as Julianne Moore's assistant on a film shooting in Ireland, and has offered to pass my script directly on to Julianne, without having to go via her agent in the US.

Every time there is the vaguest possibility of a casting, all the names have to be re-jigged to imagine how they might all work together. Casting about with these kinds of names is more akin to playing with Monopoly money than the real thing, though, as I know that the chances of her doing it are, well . . .

However, I recently saw her on an Actors' Studio programme and she came across with such great humour, warmth and integrity; she has worked with Robert Altman a couple of times, and is the rare combination of great actor *and* star, so I figure that I can't *not* give it a try. Bob Balaban assured me that actresses are so short-changed in terms of decent roles that I should be bold.

### *6 August 2003*

Fax from Julianne Moore thanking me for sending the script, saying she enjoyed it but is pretty much booked up in the months ahead. Having been burnt by the epic delay in following strict protocol and sending a script and offer to one actor at a time, *until* he/she passes on it, I opted to send it out to a list. Even if Catherine, Meg and Julianne have 'passed' on it, at least it's all happened within a few weeks. The rejections are coming thick and faster now, but their effect is mostly annulled because it really does feel like it *will* happen.

Marie-Castille sends the script to Emmanuelle Béart, who agrees to meet me. Having only seen her speak English in a small role in *Mission Impossible*, I request that she reads a couple of scenes with me to get the measure of what is possible.

# DEVELOPMENT

## 22 August 2003

Confirmation that Miranda Richardson will definitely play Lauren – my mother. All hail and hallelujah!

## 23 August 2003

Marie-Castille emails that Ms Béart will not read, but will meet me on the 29th in Paris. This is essentially all about 'accommodating' Marie-Castille in return 'payment' for her agreeing to film the Independence footage. As I have watched eight films on DVD of Emmanuelle Béart, six of which she suffers brilliantly in, and two comedies of such excruciating awfulness that *I* was suffering, it's clear to me that comedy is not her natural forte.

I brainstorm through the night trying to think of an alternative and am rewarded with the idea of Emily Watson! Send her the script pronto. Obviously she's *not* American, but she is a peerless actress, and my wife, who is a professional voice coach, assures me that Emily could do an authentic accent.

## 27 August 2003

Cate Blanchett's agent confirms that her client is booked solid through till kingdom come. Again I felt 'compromised' approaching Cate as I know her socially, my wife having coached her accents on various films.

### *29 August 2003*

6 p.m. meeting at the Hôtel Lutetia in Saint-Germain with Emmanuelle Béart. She tells me straight off the blocks that she has never heard of me, has briefly skimmed the script and has only agreed to the meeting as her agent is encouraging her to do more work in English. She added that I was very lucky to be meeting with her as she was such a huge star in France, and that she would never have met my French unknown equivalent. Fair dos. Having established her great status, I countered by asking her about *Mission Impossible*, given that it's the only role in which I had seen her speak English.

This prompts her to drop her head into her hands, saying she finds acting in a foreign language can often be an out-of-body nightmare experience. I can only agree with her and quote my *Monsieur N.* attempts. The ice is broken and it's clear she is in an emotional state. Her ex-boyfriend died recently, and she is overwhelmingly sad *and* hounded by the press. She speaks about her 'tristesse' screen persona and it is mutually agreed that we will not be working together. *Real* relief, as Ruby is the one role in the story that requires a warm, untroubled, resilient, upbeat persona.

Send the script to Juliette Binoche in the spirit of trying to keep the producer happy, but I'm almost sure she will not be interested or available.

### *6 September 2003*

Go to Swaziland with Marie-Castille, Pierre Kubel and a small crew. The reality of actually shooting makes my knees go. *Terrible* weather

– wet, misty and very cold, precisely what I don't want. We meet Qhawe Mamba, who guides us to a prime filming position directly below the balcony from where King Mswati will make his speech in the Somhlolo Stadium. Perfect. I cannot believe we are really here and have this freedom and access. Red-coated soldiers parade back and forth, as do brass bands and schoolchildren doing gymnastic displays, freezing in the mist and drizzle. There are great cheers and ululations when the King enters the packed stadium and inspects the traditionally dressed warrior regiments, wearing animal skins, beads and feathers, seemingly unchanged in over two hundred years. Except the weather makes it look like Wales with Africans.

Michael Snyman, the cameraman, does his level best to get as much footage which excludes obvious twenty-first-century cars and clothing. As the rain is relentless, I'm unsure whether we will be able to make use of it.

I sneak a few free hours to myself to wander my old haunts. Despite the schizoid nature of my childhood, divided between the good and horrendous, and the decimation of Mbabane – very run down and most of the huge old trees chopped down – nothing can erase the hypnotically charged memory capsule of my childhood. Every street, every house, every main building is quietly fizzing with characters and events that no amount of physical deterioration can dispel. It doesn't matter how often I go back, I am still drawn to revisit every haunt for a top-up, as there is always some memory that dislodges or ghosts out. I have an email friendship with Richard Clarke, who left Mbabane in 1971 when his parents emigrated to Perth – he is a fellow detailed-memory traveller, with astonishingly clear recall of that cusp between being a boy and grappling adolescence.

## 7 September 2003

Visit Jane Stephens in Pigg's Peak to have another recce of the Boshimela house, and confirmed that we will be able to film in April–May. The weather is picture-perfect today and a chorus of 'if only's' irritates my innards.

Catch a flight to Jo'burg in the early evening and then a connecting flight on to Cape Town to start a week's rehearsals and costume fittings for *Story of an African Farm*, which the producer has spent ten years trying to get off the ground. Makes my 'journey' seem snappy by comparison.

## 10 September 2003

Thank the techno-geek gods for inventing email. Despite being isolated in the Karoo desert in the middle of nowhere, I am able to keep to business as usual.

I get a message from Emily Watson to say that she thinks the script is wonderful and that her agent reckons it's the best she's read in ages.

> My interest is definitely piqued, but no notion of what next year holds for me and don't feel in a position to make commitments at the moment. But bloody well done, you, I was really impressed. And my god, was that you?

Oooh, man, this is a teaser. On the one hand approbation, on the other doubt. But this I can live with for a while.

Track the script sent to Sarah Jessica Parker and am told she is on holiday in Greece.

# DEVELOPMENT

## *16 September 2003*

Meitjiesfontein in the Karoo, three hours north-east of Cape Town. There is a Victorian hotel beside a trans-Karoo railway siding, a post office and one petrol pump. No shop, radio or TV anywhere, only a phone line which Internets me out nightly.

Quite enjoying the vast empty landscape playing a con artist trying to seduce an oversexed, hippopotamus-sized lady farmer. The South African director seems wary of me, worried that because I've worked with Altman and Co. he will not pass muster, and treats me as though I am either going to shatter like antique Venetian glass or snap his head off. In a total reversal of the usual director–actor relationship, he seeks reassurance from *me*!

The hotel menu runs the gauntlet of Karoo lamb soup, lamb cutlets, lamb stew and lamb shepherd's pie. The staff are very friendly, mostly toothless, look almost inbred and clearly regard all of us as aliens from Pluto. They cannot get their heads around us not wanting to eat three types of starch on the same plate – rice, potatoes and chips with every order.

Ah, that's rich, considering you were brought up in Mbabane, my boy, but like everything, you get institutionalized fast and work back and forth through the options with ease after a week.

## *30 September 2003*

Got a reassuring email from Julie Walters' agent to say she is still 'on board' subject to how long she would have to be apart from her daughter.

Sent the script to Charlize Theron, in the hope she might be

43

interested as she grew up just outside Jo'burg, a few hours west of Swaziland, with a violent alcoholic father, whom her mother shot dead in self-defence. She could play Ruby as either an American or a South African.

I'm certainly not giving up on Emily, but having been Fienned, I'm not taking *any* delaying chances again.

### 6 October 2003

Call from Juliette Binoche, who is doing a Brian de Palma film during our proposed shooting dates next spring, but she kindly agrees to read the script.

Marie-Castille calls to say that Gabriel Byrne's agent says the money she offered was the lowest he'd ever got and could not do it for that.

Another reality check: up until now, I've not concerned myself with the actor salaries as I'm not the producer, and wonder what Marie-Castille thought these 'name' actors I have been encouraged to chase so relentlessly *would* be expecting, low budget or not? Makes a real farce out of even *thinking* about the big star names.

### 16 October 2003

It's bizarre, standing in the night desert air under a vast canopy of stars, taking a call on a mobile from my agent in Los Angeles, who tactfully tells me about an offer to start shooting a large-budget Twentieth Century Fox remake of *Flight of the Phoenix* in Namibia from 10 November through till March next year, adding that both Stephen Rea and Robert Carlyle had turned it down, hence the late offer. Charming.

Taking this would mean I could not do my film. But with the never-never nature of it all, I run this offer past Marie-Castille, as much as anything to test how likely she, as producer, thinks that we will make it next spring. Which has the desired effect.

My American agent quotes the grim statistics for low-budget independent films never getting made, and as an agent, not unreasonably has to warn me about the unlikelihood of it happening. This only stiffens my resolve not to give up now for some dumb remake.

Sent the script to Rachel Weisz, who does a great American accent, but is probably too young opposite Gabriel, and doubtless costs upwards of $5 million. Most of the entire budget, in other words. But send it anyway.

### 27 October 2003

Agent email:

Rachel Weisz has read and likes *Wah-Wah* but does not wish to play Ruby at this time. She wishes you all the best with the film.

I'm grateful for a prompt response, even if it's a no. Jumping ages, I send it to Geena Davis.

### 6 November 2003

Back in London and off to the first casting session with potential boys at Celestia Fox's house in Clapham. As a starting point she has brought in boys who have worked professionally before. I recall a phone conversation with Alan Parker some months ago when he was visiting Bruce Robinson, who warned me that casting children can take months. As the veteran director of *Bugsy Malone*, *Fame*, *The Commitments* and *Angela's Ashes*, his advice looms ominously, and yet the first boy I meet, Zac Fox, is an immediate possibility. Zac is at the Sylvia Young Theatre School and has done a tour of *The King and I*, but no TV or film work as yet. He's very confident, assured, articulate and amenable to direction when I go through a couple of scenes with him, and speaks with a received English accent thatdoesn't sound too contemporary.

I cannot believe this has happened so fast; first out of the traps, as it were. The only problem is he could not possibly look old enough to smoke a joint or kiss a girl.

The fourth boy in is Nicholas *About a Boy* Hoult, who is only six months older than Zac, but seems four years older. Nails the part *immediately*.

Celestia thinks I am jumping every gun, and when I re-moot the idea of having two boys play the same role at different ages, she points out that they don't look remotely similar.

'But they look oddly alike,' I say.

'That's only because you *want* them to.'

She agrees to get them back to do a video screen test together next week, if only to prove me wrong! Every other boy reads perfectly well, but none get it like Zac or Nick. Am *really* excited. Plan to meet more after school hours tomorrow afternoon. Then to Eton next week.

### 13 November 2003

Meet Emily Watson at the Covent Garden Hotel to show her the location film and talk about the script. She has a million questions about everything from the emotional pitch and centre of the character through to accent details. Her instincts and emotional intelligence, if they're not the same thing, are such that I have to control myself from handcuffing her to the sofa until she signs on the dotted.

When she asks what I'm after, I borrow Bruce Robinson's directorial advice on *Withnail and I* when he demanded that the actors' commitment to the script and character be so visceral, it's as if it gets glued to the celluloid. No half-measures. Full-bodied and present. As I say this I realize I am sounding like a beer commercial. Which makes her laugh.

The fact that she has agreed to meet and see the location film is good. I have, though, also sent the script to Laura Linney – until someone commits, I *have* to do this.

### 14 November 2003

Emily sends an email saying she was inspired by my passion for the story and promises to 'get all her ducks in a row soon'. And may they all quack 'Yes', please!

### 17 November 2003

Marie-Castille is over from Paris and takes me to meet potential investors, requiring a pitch and performance not unlike the one I made in Altman's *The Player* in 1991, except this is a real-life begging-bowl process. Although there are fancy offices with secretaries, suits and phones a-ringing, it's begging all the same. The reactions of the faces are impossible to read. Clearly years of being begged have fine-tuned the investors' poker expressions. Marie-Castille is convinced it has all gone very well.

## 19 November 2003

Heart-stopper announcement in the trade press that Gabriel Byrne is set to star in an Australian film in April! I email and phone his agent. Of course he too has to keep all options open as we are not fully financed – but neither is the Australian film, I find out, so there is partial relief, although the argy-bargy between his agent and Marie-Castille about money does not help.

## 20 November 2003

Eton housemaster Simon Dormandy kindly organizes a group of boys to audition, who are suitably named Fritzi, Freddy, Nick, Bertie, Charlie and the like. The 'problem' with modern-day public-schoolboy accents is that they mostly have a smattering of mockney glottal sounds that sound very contemporary.

The boys are alarmingly self-possessed and I am momentarily wrong-footed, but once they start talking about their families and lives outside of school the seams of dysfunction are painfully present, which is what I need to tap into, and tell them all so in turn. Simon agrees to let me make a shortlist and return to tape them reading a prepared scene next week.

Celestia has the great knack of speaking to children without being patronizing and encouraging them to talk very directly. She is the greatest ally I could wish for and has resolutely stood by me through this every step of the way. Especially this week with the Gabriel and Emily 'wobbles'.

Send script to Celia Imrie for the role of Lady Riva, the British High Commissioner's gorgon of a wife and self-appointed Queen of

# DEVELOPMENT

Am-dram. Marie-Castille suggests we try Holly Hunter for role of Ruby, although her hiccup about Gabriel's asking price plants a seed of real doubt – *if* any of these American stars said yes, I wonder what she thinks they would accept in salary.

Still waiting and hoping for Emily, but know this is probably unwise and send it to Gillian Anderson, who now lives in London post her *X-Files* tenure across the pond.

### 21 November 2003

Video-test Zac Fox and Nicholas Hoult, and when they are together, Celestia relents and agrees that they are a match. I can't quite believe it has happened so fast. Nick agrees to coaching to get his accent more in line with Zac's. My real worry about finding the 'boy' is over. When I played the initial video tests to my wife and daughter, they unanimously and spontaneously chose both of them, without any word from me, which is hugely reassuring.

### 24 November 2003

Emily Watson commits to playing Ruby! Nicholas Hoult is cast to play Nicolas Cage's son in *The Weather Man* on condition he can do a believable American accent, shooting at exactly the same time as *Wah-Wah*. His agent calls my wife to coach him – ouch!

### 26 November 2003

Emily Watson withdraws for personal reasons that I am unable to tell anyone about, but which are unarguable. Really gutted. So near, so far. Will Gabriel withdraw and take another offer in hand over my bird in the bush? Three days ago I had the lead roles cast and have now lost two of them!!

### 9 December 2003

Finance on his Australian film gets delayed and, miracle of miracles, a deal is struck and Gabriel is signed to do *Wah-Wah*.

### 10 December 2003

Financial turn-downs from Pathé, Icon and the Film Council. Gillian Anderson is keen to meet and says she loves the script. My head is now fully yo-yoing with the ups and downs of this past week. If selling a house revolves around 'location, location, location', then surely the movie equivalent is 'casting, casting, casting'.

### 12 December 2003

Nicholas Hoult comes round for his accent-coaching for the Cage film, in a real push-me-pull-you state, wanting to do both, but the

Cage film is green-lit and studio financed. My wife is in the unenviable position of having to make him sound as authentic as possible to convince the head of Paramount Pictures to cast him as an American, *knowing* that her husband is climbing the walls upstairs. If successful, I have lost my lead teenage actor.

### 15 December 2003

Lunch with Gillian Anderson, who is all compliments about the script. I discover she lives with Julian Ozanne, whose sister I was at school with in Swaziland. Gillian is beautiful, open, articulate, exudes warmth – and crucially wants to play Ruby!

### Christmas 2003

Escape to the heat of Cape Town and meet up with Bob Geldof and his family. He asks how my film is progressing, and when I express doubts, he adamantly informs me that it will happen. He'd make the perfect film producer if he wasn't saving the world. None of us has made plans for New Year's Eve, and everywhere is booked solid. But Bob being Bob, restless as a quiver, he not only manages to get a glass-walled private room in a beachside restaurant for sixteen people, but wheedles a discount out of them to boot. Bono and his family join us, and at midnight the gob-smacked clientele are treated to an impromptu free 'gig' by the Dublin duo. A very good start to 2004!

### 3 January 2004

Topsy-turvied by the news that Emily Watson's personal circumstances, which had prompted her withdrawal, have now changed and
she is available and keen to play Ruby. This is great New Year news.
Having tried for so long to cast this role, to have *two* actresses on
board now is not a happy quandary, however. I will have to prostrate
and beg Gillian Anderson's forgiveness and withdraw my offer to
her. Unfortunately she is travelling in Africa and unreachable until
the 20th, so I resort to apologetic emails and phone messages to her
agent.

I can't quite believe I now have Gabriel *and* Emily *and* Miranda
*and* Julie!

### 5 January 2004

Purple email to Emily:

THANK YOU for agreeing to play Ruby and coming aboard our
African ride. I have been *levitating* ever since speaking to you and
could not be more thrilled if I tried. You are so perfect for the part
and it is an absolute forty carat gold bling-bling sparkly jump up
and down on the sofa privilege and delight for me that you have
agreed to do it.

I have offered Celia Imrie the choice of playing either June or
Lady Riva Hardwick. The former is the more sympathetic role,
whereas Riva is a leviathan. My belief in her talent is such that she
could play either role equally well but I'm hoping she opts for Riva,

as it is a part that would require considerable steeliness, as opposed to the natural warmth and empathy that exudes from her. I know all too acutely how frustrating it is to be typecast, and discussed this with Celia at length.

### *6 January 2004*

Celia confirms she will play Lady Riva, and Julian Wadham agrees to play Charles – colonial grandee and pompously fluent speaker of *Wah-Wah*. After so many moons of feeling like I was getting nowhere fast, it really does seem tangible that filming will actually happen in April after all.

Brace myself for phone calls to the BBC, Film Four and the Film Council requesting another 'look' at the script in view of the cast now attached. Polite agreement generally, but Tessa Ross from Film Four warns that it was a very long shot as they only finance eight films a year and everything has to be youth-orientated, cutting-edge stuff. Likewise, David Thompson at the BBC says they already have three African-based projects slated, so thinks it highly unlikely mine would get a look-in.

### *11 January 2004*

Evening call to Gillian Anderson in Africa, having managed to track her down via her agent. I'd anticipated she'd give me a verbal lathering for my U-turn, but being the person she is, she is saintly in her understanding of my predicament. Having been so conscience-stricken and anxious to speak to her directly, she could not have been more generous and understanding if she had tried. Resolve to find some way in the future to make good her faith in me with some reciprocal gesture.

Psychic relief.

## 12 January 2004

Nicholas Hoult has landed the role in *The Weather Man*, which shoots for two months from late February till end of April. However, his start dates are not set in stone yet, so I hang on to the wispy hope that I can still cast him, *if* we shoot at the end of April as planned, *if* his dates don't get delayed or changed. *If* I had a pound for every *if* during this whole process . . . *if* only.

Speak to Gabriel Byrne about considering dropping a few pounds if possible as his character dies at the end of the story – extremely delicate stuff as he is not exactly overweight, but have to ask anyway. He jauntily emails that he has lost weight since we met and 'should be a shadow of my porker self by the time you see me next!' His accessibility and good humour bode very well for what lies ahead, and keeping in regular email contact with him in New York will hopefully pave the path to real familiarity by the time we start shooting.

## 13 January 2004

Kate Buckley, Nick Hoult's agent, calls to say she hopes to have a final shooting schedule for him by the end of the week. I ask Sheena Napier to design the costumes, as she grew up in Egypt in the sixties and is very familiar with the colonial look of the period, as well as having connected with the script at an emotional level. She comes highly recommended by John Bright, who owns Cosprop, the costume-hire company. Ask Karen Jones to do script continuity and supervision as I liked her so much from working with her on *Hound of the Baskervilles*. I have kept lists down the years of all the crew I really admired and enjoyed working with, in the hope that I would one day be able to work with them on my own film.

### 14 January 2004

George Lys, who despite having left Swaziland is still connected to the King, requests that we supply him with as much info as possible about the number of work permits we will need for cast and crew, as well as cargo-entry permits for equipment trucks, way in advance of our next planned location recce in February.

Send script and offer to play June to Fenella Woolgar, whom I met on Stephen Fry's *Bright Young Things*. She is the right class, highly intelligent and might delight in playing June in all her faux-pas-ridden stupidity. She's also be a perfect match for Julian Wadham's Charles, with whom she has to cop off. Both actors have marvellously beaky profiles and a gift for pompous comedy.

Mid-morning panic phone call from Marie-Castille to say that the Stephens family's lawyer in Jo'burg has rejected the offer to rent Boshimela, our main house location. Will I call and try and reason with him? This is a gut-plunger as it is not really my job, but specifically the producer's call.

I phone the lawyer, who is extremely angry at how insultingly low the offer is, since which time he has made enquiries about going rates for filming and come up with a figure that is astronomical in terms of our budget. He has been quoted rates for shooting a commercial which are always very high and usually only require two or three days' house rental at most. He has multiplied this rate over the five weeks we need for filming, hence the astro figure. If he had been properly briefed and provided with comparative filming rates by the South African line producer in the first place, *none* of this nonsense would have arisen. He also says the line producer was difficult, that he will not deal with her ever again and will negotiate only via me.

Oh, brother. Just what I need right now.

I dig out old crew info and call a production manager in Cape Town to get written confirmation of the going filming rates, so that the lawyer can be reassured as to a reasonable fee – which turns out to be three times higher than the producer's initial offer. Write an email to Glenda Stephens to try and suss out if the demanded rental price is a 'scare' tactic or whether there is still hope to secure this crucial location.

Email from Emily Watson asking what she should do about her hair, as it's currently long and blonde and what did I have in mind? In light of all the other hassles, I feel inordinately excited to be discussing Emily's hair requirements. In a single day, the sheer variety of questions is a yo-yo of extremes. Julian Wadham calls for a lengthy discussion of what kind of moustache he should grow to play Charles. Surreal to be talking about these details with the parallel universe of house rentals, Nick Hoult's availability and the big 'If' of whether we will get financed in time to shoot at the end of April. Mirages and mirrors.

### 15 January 2004

Long phone calls back and forth with the Stephens' lawyer, who seems perfectly reasonable and now understands the difference between shooting an advert and a feature film; he will put all this to the Stephens family and get back to me once they have made a decision either way.

Marie-Castille is adamant that he is crazy, but I do my best to explain that whether she thinks him crazy or not is irrelevant as we need the house location and cannot afford to alienate them any further. In other words, pay what they have settled on and shut up.

She also requested that I try and get discounted rates from Sir Richard Branson on flights to Africa, as I have met him a few times and know his sister. Begging-bowl time, but I understand that at worst, he can just say no. Which he doesn't, instead asking for crew and cast numbers as well as cargo requirements!

Barnaby Thompson, from Fragile Films, who produced *Spice World* and is now co-owner of Ealing Studios, calls having read the script. He is full of compliments and enthusiastic that he can secure English financing. I put him in touch with Marie-Castille.

## 20 January 2004

Noon meeting in Soho with Marie-Castille and Gabriel's agent Teri Hayden, over from Dublin, to discuss his deal and reassure her that the film is actually going to happen. Meet with costume designer Sheena Napier. Marie-Castille essentially asks her to tap dance for the job I have already asked her to do, with much high-falutin' yak about design statement and concept, quoting *Far from Heaven*, Todd Haynes's highly stylized, camp film set in the fifties, as a reference point for the look of *Wah-Wah*!

Neither Sheena nor I are prepared for this and the meeting is extremely sticky. The costume budget is so tiny that it would barely cover the making of half Julianne Moore's wardrobe for the Solenz film. There's a weird contradiction at play – Oscar-nominated Sheena, with all her contacts and experience, is being evaluated by a relatively inexperienced producer with only one French film to her credit, which flopped badly.

Every day now is non-stop questions, meetings, emails, rejections, reinstatements, quibbles, vacillations, rewrites et al., but I'm really thriving on all the activity and having my negotiating muscles stretched. As nervous as I am about my inexperience, and without wanting to sound like a self-help guru, I feel charged and motivated to give of my very best.

No word on the Boshimela house yet.

### 25 January 2004

Receive an email from Marie-Castille regarding the Virgin flight deal that makes me blush. Although I spent considerable energy at her behest securing an extremely generous and favourable deal on flights and cargo from Virgin, and assigned a designated phone number and assistant to deal specifically with all our requirements, she now says her deal with British Airways is better and asks if I'm willing to go back to Sir Richard Branson and try and get him to lower his offer.

I feel shamed that she could ask me to do this and suggest she make the call herself. Wish I had never agreed to call him in the first place . . . I can't avoid the sense that my goodwill is being used by her for these flights and on the house-rental farrago. *Very* uncomfortable. I have ended up with the responsibility of having to negotiate my way out of this. My wife advises me to steer clear of all this producer business and leave it to Marie-Castille, although I'm left with no alternative when, having done so, I then get landed with having to sort things out. Really worrying, and does not portend well.

## 26 January 2004

Meet Michael Pickwoad, the bow-tie-wearing production designer of *Withnail and I* and *How to Get Ahead in Advertising*. It's a very strange reversal of roles interviewing *him* as a prospective crew member; I feel inadequate, and say so. He enthuses about the script, has a multitude of design ideas and is as personable as ever I remember. I call Marie-Castille after the meeting and say Michael is the man for the job, but she insists on seeing his show-reel first. Again, *her* CV does not bear scrutiny compared to the highly experienced professionals she is appraising, but suspect this is all to do with her holding out for having French costume and production designers instead, and she is just humouring me. Whichever and whatever, her reluctance to communicate is frustrating.

Sheena Napier emails a basic budget breakdown of what she estimates hiring and making costs will be, with the proviso that as she thought the meeting with Marie-Castille 'was not a huge success', her agent was putting her up for other work. Sheena generously agrees to pursue her research and sourcing of vintage clothing, until she hears otherwise.

## 27 January 2004

Email Marie-Castille's new assistant, Laurence, to try and get deals and contracts secured for Sheena Napier and Karen Jones to avoid losing them to other films. Getting any quick response is proving difficult. Our 'regular' emails have significantly dwindled since the Boshimela house deal cock-up.

## 28 January 2004

Rejection letter from Tessa Ross at Film Four, couched in praise for the script and cast but with the anticipated 'our remit right now is very contemporary, and sadly we cannot come on board'.

*Finally* some good news from the Stephens' lawyer – although they want a higher price for the house rental than the going rate for an exclusive Cape Town mansion, as opposed to an isolated house in the Swazi countryside, most importantly we are negotiating and have not been turned down outright. Having had to salvage the first round of messed-up negotiations myself, I email Marie-Castille to take over the deal-making responsibility again as this is producer's territory, requesting that she does so *prior* to our being in the house for the planned recce in a couple of weeks' time. This is the first time I have ended an email with 'Best regards' rather than the usual 'Lots of love'.

For me there seems a clear pattern now – when things go wrong at her end, I am called upon to try and fix them up. This is fast dissolving the necessary mutual trust.

## 29 January 2004

My American agent calls to ask if I am available to be a 'guest star' in the final double episode of *Frasier* playing one of Daphne's long-lost brothers, shooting for a week in mid-March.

*The Weather Man* shooting schedule is finally released and reveals that Nicholas Hoult won't be free until after 15 May, making him unavailable to us. Yet another stomach plunge; call Celestia Fox to start the search for lead role of teenage Ralph all over again.

## 30 January 2004

*Still* no response from Marie-Castille, and I'm getting more calls from the Stephens' lawyer. I call Glenda Stephens and her husband Dr John direct, and they mercifully hear me out and agree to the lower price that correlates to the equivalent rental in Cape Town. In other words, a substantial amount, but something that the budget can realistically accommodate.

Laurence, the new assistant, sends this charming but unintentionally funny email:

I am cheerful to work on *Wah-Wah* and join forces to your on this film.

We are booked to fly to Swaziland for a location recce on 14 February with a production designer we still don't have.

## 3 February 2004

Having had zero response from Marie-Castille I brace myself, call her, and for once get through. She says that she senses I do not trust her anymore – to which I reply that I am *trusting* her to produce the film of my own life story, *want* to trust her, but need to share as much information as possible, so that I don't end up chasing after her the whole time.

She dismissed Michael Pickwoad on the grounds that he had too many TV design credits compared to his film credits! She then promptly suggested two French designers. I countered by demanding to be sent their CVs. Doesn't make sense – an English designer will have contacts with props houses in London and have a better knowledge of the British colonial look.

When I ask her about the lack of follow-up regarding essential key crew member deals (production and costume designer and script supervisor/continuity), she finally reveals after much goading that she was hoping to employ mostly French crew as they are cheaper.

When I asked why she did not spell this out from the beginning, thus enabling me to avoid wasting my time interviewing people in London, there was deep silence. And a 'Well, that's just the way it is, my *dear* Richard' that bore all the hallmarks of a spurned teenager. This was confirmed when she said she was hurt by my 'Best regards' email endings as opposed to 'Lots of love'.

Yee-ha, Trigger. It's come down to *that*. If she can afford to concern herself with this tiny detail, how in hell does she manage to avoid the *real* issues of getting a crew in time? I tell her that I will continue to meet English production designers. At least we have both aired things, and I email her with the usual 'lol' ending in an attempt to go forward positively, while also urging her to keep me informed and to respond to emails and calls.

### 4 February 2004

Meet designer Gary Williamson, a Northern Irishman who has the gift of the gab. He brings a huge portfolio of his collaboration with Dennis Potter and sketches of his ideas having read the script. He also happens to have worked in France for a French director and I think this will tip him into Marie-Castille's favour. He also just happens to be married to Chrissie Baker, the make-up and hair artist who does all Julie Walters' films and TV work. A married couple double-working whammy partnership that is very attractive. It means they can share a hotel room, adding to my fuel to employ them over a French designer. Gary is also available to travel to Swaz in a week's time.

## 6 February 2004

I contact Anthony Frewin, who has written *Colour Me Kubrick*, in which I have been cast to play a cameo role, to request permission from the Kubrick estate to license a clip from *A Clockwork Orange* which I want to use. He is instantly helpful and replies that 'the *Clockwork* droogs in Swaziland rather appeals to me'.

## 9 February 2004

So far Marie-Castille has not made contact with Barnaby Thompson at Fragile Films, despite his attempts to reach her. This is confounding, as she asked me to try and find financial support wherever I can and Barnaby came out of the starting gates at full speed.

At her behest, I go to meet the guys at Redbus Productions to pitch my film in the hope that they will distribute it, having been turned down by every other distributor we previously tried in London.

5 p.m. call from Marie-Castille who says she has finally spoken to Barnaby and that Redbus had called to say how well my meeting with them had gone. This is a *start*.

No French designers are available at this last-minute notice, and having checked out Gary's work on the French film he did, Marie-Castille agrees to employ him as well as Chrissie. *Progress!*

# THE WAH-WAH DIARIES

## 11 February 2004

Doomsday legislation for the British film industry – the government has closed a loophole in existing film taxation that has instantly shut down twenty-five films. *Pole-axed*. All I can hear in my head is John Malkovich repeatedly intoning, 'It is beyond my control. It is beyond my control. It is beyond my control,' from *Dangerous Liaisons*. Called Scion Films to find out if they have gone down, and by some miracle they haven't and are still on as co-producers. Fend off calls and emails all day from agents and actors asking if *Wah-Wah* has collapsed, everyone assuming it has.

Feel like my spine is buckling. Big names and bestseller titles have gone down, and I cannot quite believe we are still hanging in there.

To Celestia Fox's office to see a new boy, George Clarke, for role of Ralph. He tests really strongly and we resolve that he is the best alternative to Nick Hoult. Very hard to give up on Nick, though, and having been through this once already with Emily Watson, I feel guilty at trying to find someone else. Feel exhausted by this up-down-and-sideways emotional heave-ho. Now it's on, then it's off, then on again, then tottering in all directions.

## 12 February 2004

Marie-Castille emails to say that Redbus will distribute the film, which is fantastic news and means we can go back to the Film Consortium, who will put up ten per cent of the budget on condition that we have a distributor. Good news after the very frightening news yesterday. However, any chance of Barnaby Thompson raising finances in this sledge-hammered situation is finito, and he generously apologizes for not being able to help us out any more.

Despite the tax cataclysmics, we have secured the main cast, production, costume and make-up designers, and finally a distributor.

George Lys in Swaziland confirms that the cast and crew will require work permits, application forms and medical certificates and estimates two to three weeks to process all this before we can start shooting. Forewarned – forearmed. All these details are emailed to Marie-Castille. And phone-messaged as well. My twin obsessions since we began working together have been to secure work permits well in advance as well as song-rights clearances for *Camelot*.

We have to keep young George Clarke on hold till Marie-Castille has seen his screen test when we return from the recce on 23 February. But he is very excited to have been chosen, and is a very good actor.

### 13 February 2004

Email from Marie-Castille:

> Shockwave has touched French film industry as well. Credit committee on *Wah-Wah* was cancelled yesterday because of it. Scion has been reassuring but banks need to have official explanation and reassurance. Let's have a great recce and move forward. I will call make-up person when I return. There is no urgency.

### *21 February 2004*

The week's recce was a real triumph. Gary Williamson lathered up the producers with his charm and between him, Pierre Aïm the cinematographer, and the first assistant director Valerie Othnin-Girard, we got every location nailed down and plotted out. Met the King again, who gave blessings and permission to film wherever we wanted to, after which we nosed out a fleet of vintage cars owned by an aficionado called A.D. Van Wyk, willing to help us out with sixties Mercedes-Benzes, old Land Rovers and a pillar-box-red sports car with left-hand drive for Ruby. Booked local cricket teams and warrior regiments and got amazing cooperation in a rush around to get everything done in six days, including a brilliant afternoon in close proximity to a herd of elephants. Spent a day in Jo'burg with local casting director to sign up actors for smaller roles.

Got home to discover a fax from Warner Brothers granting permission to use the clip from *A Clockwork Orange*.

All hunky-dory and on course to start shooting 3 May.

### *4 March 2004*

Gary Williamson reports back on his production meeting in Paris, at which Marie-Castille and Pierre Kubel gave him the A–Z of the hierarchy of the film, emphasizing how important they were as producers at the top of the pyramid, which made us laugh. Gary has worked on more films than either of them will produce in what's left of their lifetimes! Such is his good nature, he shrugged it off, amused that they felt the need to do this in the first place. He is due to fly out to start pre-production on 15 March. When he asked in the meeting about who would be coordinating actors, costumes, make-up tests and wig fittings in England, he was told that all this could be arranged via Paris!

## 8 March 2004

Maggie Rodford, the agent to composer Patrick Doyle and film music supervisor at Air-Edel studios in London, calls to reiterate that securing the *Camelot* song rights clearances well in advance of shooting is essential, and will email and call Marie-Castille.

## 10 March 2004

Pre-production meeting in Paris at which Marie-Castille announced that song rights would be thirty per cent cheaper if done via France. When I asked for specifics of why and how this could possibly be the case, she told me not to get involved and to keep out of this; she would deal with it.

Called Maggie Rodford immediately on my return and her undisguised scepticism set all my alarm bells ringing. Maggie assured me that global song rights were pretty standard and she could not begin to understand how negotiating them via France could work out so much cheaper.

## 11 March 2004

As Marie-Castille is suddenly keen to try and rework the schedule around getting Nick Hoult back on board, I track down Todd Black, the producer of *The Weather Man*, who says they are still on schedule: Nick will complete at the end of April and has one blue-screen special-effects day in Chicago to film mid-May. In theory, we could start shooting with Zac Fox, his younger version, and work around these dates. But it is a huge risk if their schedule shifts. I email George Clarke's family, explain my dilemma and ask for their patience.

Maggie does some research on the *Camelot* clearances and confirms that they will have to go through the American offices and that there is no precedent of costs being thirty per cent lower done via France. Brick-wall frustration, and the song-rights problem gnaws away at the back of my neck.

### 12 March 2004

Valerie, the first assistant director who is doing the schedule, suggests we delay shooting to start on 13 May to ensure Nick Hoult's dates. Meanwhile, I spend the afternoon screen-testing a shortlist of ten further younger versions of George Clarke.

Gary and I have a last-minute meeting before he goes to start pre-production in Swaziland, and we go through myriad design, prop and furniture details. He sends a follow-up email saying, 'Remember to pack the contents of your house and bring it all to Swaziland!'

Email Gabriel Byrne, who is filming in Russia, asking if he would be able to start shooting on 13 May so that we can have Nick Hoult on board.

## *15 March 2004*

Read-through for the final episode of *Frasier* at Paramount Studios. It's nerve-racking surrounded by sixty executives, writers and actors crammed into a small room – almost every line of dialogue is rewarded with near-hysterical laughter and there's no doubting the emotional charge. It's the end of their sixteen-year run and as the last line is read, people are in floods. Especially the men, which I have never witnessed before, *anywhere*. Not even at a funeral.

It's strange to be in this homogenized mini-world with no emotional connection to me whatsoever, whilst all around nostalgia is pumping through everyone's veins at force ten. The overwhelming friendliness and camaraderie is Haägen-Dazs thick.

Already miss my family like mad, and realize that I will never really get used to this going-away-to-work stuff.

## *17 March 2004*

Email from Marie-Castille! – says her meetings in London 'have not gone great' and that the Film Consortium will not come in for ten per cent after all. She is cryptic about details, saying only that 'they are requiring things that to me are quite unacceptable' and I instantly recall similar language with regard to doing a deal on Boshimela. She signs off hollowly with 'I am hoping for the best'. Profound unease.

Maggie Rodford copies me in on the email she sends to Marie-Castille in which she diplomatically points out that song-rights clearances have to be done through the US offices of Warner Chappell and that in her experience, French music-publishing offices are 'very slow' to respond. Right now, the music clearances I am so concerned about are, I suspect, not at the top of Marie-Castille's list of priorities.

Steve Martin, whose poolside guest house I'm staying in, has translated and adapted an obscure German farce/melodrama titled *The Underpants* which we go to the opening night of at a theatre in Westwood. Sort of *Young Frankenstein* crossed with a school play. In the audience were Steven Spielberg, Kate Capshaw, Michelle Pfeiffer, Eddie Izzard, Eric Idle, Blake Edwards and Dame Julie Andrews.

That Hollywood moment is always so bizarre, when you find yourself in close proximity to a cast list that could never feasibly be in the same movie together. Yet here they all are talking to one another, as though they might be! Unlike a teenage movie audience, this theatre crowd resembles a convention of facelifts, nearlifts and Stannah stairlifts.

With *Wah-Wah* financials a-wobbling, all my brain can do is compute the collective wealth gathered in this foyer. I want to bellow out, 'Please can we have some of your dough? You wouldn't even notice a couple of hundred thousand bucks here and there, would ya?' Instead I focus on meeting Dame Julie Andrews, who valiantly manages not to slap my face which has regressed to that of a gawping *Sound of Music/Mary Poppins* eight-year-old fan.

### 18 March 2004

*Frasier* rehearsals. The resident dog farted and twenty people scattered in an instant, then it topped it off by doing a prolonged volcanic shit in the middle of the wedding-room set which cleared the whole studio for a good fifteen minutes.

I have been flown out here for eleven lines of dialogue, and suspect they might all be cut as there are fourteen writers on the show.

Flicked through ninety-nine TV channels of consumerist mayhem and got fixated by the shopping channel whilst trying to fall asleep. Two adults talked for forty-seven minutes *non-stop* about a $99 diamond-and-emerald-encrusted ring. Their improvisatory invention left me staggered and grateful to be lying down. The coup de grâce? 'It's pure fourteen-carat gold, and *that's five more than nine*'!

Checked my emails in the middle of the night and there was a cryptic message to call Marie-Castille urgently.

### *19 March 2004*

Nothing has prepared me for her news. The Rand Merchant Bank, responsible for a substantial part of the budget, has withdrawn. She is teary when she tells me this.

My mouth dries, I choke and my knees buckle as I slump to the floor. Numbly read the email from Joel Phiri, the South African co-producer at IMG, mooting details about risk assessment, sales estimates, requisite cover and the bank being unable to justify their investment sitting behind a GAP of one million euros without equity or pre-sales – all unknown quantities to me – and the conclusion: 'It will be impossible to marry RMB funding with any GAP financing. Sorry to be the bearer of such bad news. In its current shape, IMG cannot be involved in this project'.

*Shape, project, GAP.* O.H. F.U.C.K.

Marie-Castille signs off saying she will fly out to Jo'burg and see what she can salvage. Read the email she has sent to the Rand Merchant Bank, which begins with a familiar sentence: 'I was just about to write you an email today for the first time in a very long time when I got an official email from Joel Phiri.'

Having been told to keep my nose out of the financials, I had naively assumed that when we were in Swaziland and Jo'burg for the recce a month ago, Marie-Castille would have been in contact with the Rand Merchant Bank as we were about to start pre-production. She was always on her mobile and I *assumed* she was dealing with the bank.

Her epic email suggests that she has not been in recent direct contact with Rand but has rather been going through IMG. Begging the question for me, *why?* It appears that the bank has asked her to communicate through IMG and she 'explains' to the bank that she 'did not write before because we have a relationship of open communication and trust'. At this point her idea of what constitutes 'communication and trust' differs from mine. Maybe she has been on to IMG every day, but I cannot understand how we have got ourselves into this dreadful position.

She goes on to acknowledge that she had heard that the film had to go through a more official Bank process to consolidate its financing, but that *in principle* they were 'in'.

She points out that the issue RMB have raised now was *always* known to them and finishes by asking if a solution can be found.

I read, reread and read again and again this gruesome news. I am convinced that Marie-Castille has made assumptions about the financial commitment from the bank that she probably should not have. I don't know what communication has passed between her and IMG on this issue but the bottom line is that as of now we are in deep shit.

Feel like I'm dead but breathing. Lurch into the *Frasier* rehearsals and zombie my way through the day, dinner and dazed weekend ahead.

Lie wide awake counting up the list of friends who are multimillionaires and the pair of billionaires I know as well, *knowing* that to beg for movie money is the ultimate no-no. Tantamount to incest. Ghastly, *ghastly* stalemate, so near yet so far. Outside, the fairy lights in Steve's garden twinkle in the midnight breeze.

# DEVELOPMENT

## *20 March 2004*

Steve Martin, my wife and Gary Williamson all give their appraisal of Marie-Castille's email to the bank and come up with the same conclusion. Which gives me no comfort whatsoever. As Gary is the most immediately affected – he is due to fly out to start pre-production – he is the only crew member that Marie-Castille has called. He is devastated, and declares that 'assumption is the mother of all fuck-ups'. Feel utterly helpless. Steve is philosophical and quotes the stop-start syndrome his film *Shopgirl* has suffered. Gary concludes that 'if by some miracle she can still pull it together after meeting the bank next week, maybe she will be more collaborative and listen to her director in future'.

Which made me laugh out loud. Like Boris Karloff.

## *21 March 2004*

In desperation, I email a begging letter to the Rand Merchant Bank in the hope that *something* might be salvaged.

Mountain-bike ride in the steep Hollywood Hills off Mulholland Drive with Steve.

## *23 March 2004*

Dear Marie-Castille – not heard from you – please let me know where you are and what's happening. Lots of love, Richard

I am going to Jo'burg on Thursday [25th]. Until then, nothing . . . Love, Marie-Castille

Evening email from Celestia Fox firming up all the actors' contract requirements and altered shooting dates. It's unbearable to read and I shake my head in disbelief that we have finally got this close and now it's paralysed.

Celia Imrie's dates are starting to clash with her *Nanny McPhee* filming dates, while Fenella Woolgar is contracted to *Rome* and her dates could be affected. But otherwise everyone else is still available, most importantly Nick Hoult.

Count the hours till Thursday's meeting, crossing fingers, thumbs, toes and didgeridoos.

*Frasier* recording passes in a haze. Feel totally disembodied, wondering why they haven't fired me or at least asked for their money back.

### 25 March 2004

Back in London and Nicholas Hoult comes round for an accent-coaching session with my wife. I feel like some terrible traitor sitting on this secret, whilst talking him through the script. But pretending somehow helps temporarily displace the reality that at this moment in time there is no film.

6.06 p.m. email from Virginie at Loma Nasha in Paris:

I just talk with Marie-Castille she was at the airport at the end of her mobile's battery – she will call you tomorrow, but asks me to tell you that things went well and there is hope.

# DEVELOPMENT

## 26 March 2004

Marie-Castille finally calls and says she has negotiated a stay of execution and that the Rand Merchant Bank are reconsidering, whilst Coficine, the private French investment company cash-flowing the film, will also have to be appeased, but that as of now, the start date, *if we get the green light*, will be delayed by a month. Each company has to renegotiate and this will take time. Incredible temporary relief.

She has asked me to come to Paris next week for a meeting with her and Pierre Kubel. Meanwhile Valerie, the first assistant director, has withdrawn as she has another job offer in Australia and cannot afford to take the risk of *Wah-Wah* not going ahead. As she has drawn up the shooting schedule and been on the location recces, this is an undeniable blow, but in the light of everything else, par for the course now.

Call all the actors' agents and the English crew members to tell them about the month's delay. Karen Jones is now able to take another script-supervising job in the gap. Email the Swaziland Theatre Club about the delay and can well imagine their scepticism that we will *ever* actually turn up.

But actually being able to do something, after the week of inertia, is good.

The *one* advantage of the tax change and collapse of so many films is that none of the cast are being tempted away onto other projects. As of today, that is.

To say that my wife and daughter have been put through quadruple spin dry and multiple somersaults whilst standing by and supporting me throughout this debacle is to merely *hint* at the level of their love and inestimable fortitude.

## 30 March 2004

Paris lunch meeting with Marie-Castille and Pierre Kubel. My agenda is to get as clear a breakdown as possible of the budget and, most important of all, to establish a rule that she and I email/speak to one another every two days, as I had originally asked her to do when we were on the Swazi recce, but which never happened. I take a mini-tape recorder so that I cannot be accused of not remembering or misunderstanding.

Things start frostily and then go Arctic. I begin by asking for a breakdown of percentages of where the money was coming from, 'assuming' that RMB and Coficine were still participating. Much humming and ha'ing, but wait with pen poised, till finally some figures are announced: Scion thirty-three per cent, RMB thirty-three per cent, Coficine twenty-three per cent, Film Consortium ten per cent. With Film Consortium out, there is an immediate shortfall of eleven per cent. The RMB requires re-negotiations with Coficine, with whom she has a meeting this Thursday, 1 April.

When I ask why the RMB were only emailed by her *after* they had withdrawn, she points out that the RMB have asked her to go through IMG. 'But you are the overall producer,' I remind her. She threatens me by claiming that she nearly didn't go to Jo'burg last week because I had sent a begging email to the RMB, and accuses me of always trying to find fault with her and fixating on details.

Pierre Kubel chimes in and defends her, saying that she deals in big broad strokes and that I am an actor with too much time on my hands, obsessing about details and communicating! I restrain myself from breaking a plate over the stupid cunt's face.

Take a *very* deep breath and retort that it is precisely the lack of detailed follow-through and communication that is causing me so much frustration; that *without* details, we would not be up to speed with schedules, rewrites, actors' dates or locations. Maybe it was the *lack* of detail and broad-stroke assumption that led to the fracas over the Boshimela house rental and current withdrawal of the RMB.

'I don't feel you trust me,' she says.

'Marie-Castille, how do you expect me to when I am kept out of the loop? I have had a total of three emails and three phone calls from you in the past five and a half weeks.'

'There you are again with *details*.'

'We agreed at the end of the last recce that we would communicate a minimum of every two days. This has not happened. It is not only me, everyone I deal with in London says the same thing – you simply do not return calls or emails.'

I appeal to Pierre to illuminate this and he huffs and puffs and reluctantly admits that 'Marie-Castille is not a big communicator or emailer'.

'And yet you are on your mobile constantly.'

'You have to trust me.'

'You have to earn my trust, because when I have trusted you, things have not been followed through, and I have had to clear up after you.'

It's at this point I plonked the tape recorder on the table and thought she was going to hit me. 'This way I will be able to prove, if need be, that I am not making this stuff up. Did we not agree in Jo'burg to talk every couple of days?'

Kubel attempts a Kofi Annan and says, 'Maybe Marie-Castille did not understand ze English.'

'Don't give me that bullshit, Pierre, we all *perfectly* understood the arrangement, which simply has not been followed through. Unlike your offices, I am operating as a one-man-band cum line-producer in London. *Every* query comes via me when people get zero response from Marie-Castille.'

He retorts that I have to accept that she will not reply to things and that I simply have to trust her.

'Marie-Castille, is there a reason why you choose to keep me in the dark?'

'Yes, to protect you.'

This made me laugh. 'But I am *not* protected. Can you not understand that?'

She blathered on about my not trusting her and how debilitating this was, to which I said the solution is very simple – 'Tell me what's going on, reply and respond to people's calls and emails and this will all resolve itself. And as the French crew knew about Valerie's withdrawal, it might have been a courtesy to let the director know at the same time.'

I held her face in both hands on leaving, kissed her and said that no matter what, I hoped we would be able to look each other in the eye and keep talking till the film opened.

Whilst she Goliaths in 'broad strokes' and big issues, I *know* that my true strength lies in the small Davids and the crucial details.

### 31 March 2004

The all new communicating Marie-Castille will be put to the test today as the Stephens' lawyer has heard that the film has been delayed, tried to get in touch with Marie-Castille, not got through and emails me about the house deposit due on 1 April. I pass it on to Marie-Castille, who emails him, changing the deal, saying that she will not pay any deposit until she knows if the film is happening or not. The lawyer also reveals that the house is already leased out to German engineers from the beginning of July for five months! I resolve to send the ten per cent deposit myself as an act of goodwill towards the Stephens family, as they have been buggered about so much already. It seems the least I can do at the moment.

# DEVELOPMENT

## 1 April 2004

I email Marie-Castille and leave her a phone message wishing her 'great good luck and good fortune' trying to get Coficine to accommodate the RMB's proposals in her meeting with them today.

## 2 April 2004

Very curt email from Marie-Castille saying that Coficine had come up with counter-demands to the RMB. Another hurry-up-and-wait game as they ping-pong back and forth, but if they are still negotiating, there is still *hope*, boy! It feels like slow water torture, though – no sleep and that incipient dread that it will all just unravel away. I feel impotent and suspended, yo-yoing, yet I walk, talk and outwardly 'function'.

Email from Peter Capaldi cheers me no end:

Have you started? For all I know you are standing knee-deep in zebra shit commanding Swazi warriors to follow your orders. Or are you feeling that vomit-inducing flickering in the stomach, soon to be followed by the Alzheimer mental chaos as you realize the amount of answers you have to provide far exceeds the capacity of your brain to carry them at any one time, and that the tensile strength of the human skull is surprisingly great, particularly when pressure is exerted from within?

### 6 April 2004

Total silence from our great communicator. Have mown the lawn, cleaned the windows inside and out, climbed the walls, weeded, planted, repotted, cooked, biked, lap-topped and taken the dog to the vet to have twenty-two teeth removed. Could well have done with the anaesthetic myself.

### 7 April 2004

Huw Jones, who was in the last Colonial Secretariat in Swaziland, emails that he has just received a batch of Super 8mm films from Jann and Alistair Smart which includes colour footage of the Independence ceremony and possibly my father's OBE ceremony! Would it be of use? You bet!

Offered the villain role in Steve Martin's remake of *The Pink Panther* shooting in Paris this summer. Doesn't bear thinking about yet till I know about *my* flick.

### 9 April 2004

Trudie Styler generously gives me a list of contacts to try and secure our missing ten per cent of finance, but warns that anyone coming in at this late stage will not be happy about being repaid last in the queue. At this point, it's all semantics anyway.

### 19 April 2004

Haggard with waiting. Four weeks since everything went belly-up. Not a *squeak* of news. Nada! Our last-chance start date of 7 June is an alarming seven weeks away.

Trying to reassure all the cast and crew to hang in there whenever they call in to check what's happening is a white-knuckle ride.

The Stephens family trustees accept the goodwill cash deposit from me.

### 20 April 2004

Call and email Marie-Castille to no avail to say that Emily Watson is about to bail out. She finally calls back and says she has a meeting with Coficine tomorrow afternoon. Resolve to make a shortlist and check availabilities of first assistant directors in London, *just in case*.

### 21 April 2004

Casting director Mary Selway dies. She gave me my first film role and started casting this film four years ago – very sad to lose her feisty and fearless presence.

## 23 April 2004

Read *Hamlet* – a man caught betwixt and between if ever there was one. His penultimate thoughts fit perfectly:

> *If it be now, 'tis not to come;*
> *If it be not now, yet it will come: the readiness is all.*
> *Since no man knows aught of what he leaves,*
> *What is't to leave betimes?*
> *Let be.*

5.30 p.m. call from Marie-Castille. The film is fully financed and will start shooting on 7 June! Levitated.

Immediately send her an email for the record:

Dear Marie-Castille,
FELICITATIONS!!
CONGRATULATIONS!!
I AM IN TOTAL SHOCK, TOTALLY THRILLED, UNBELIEVABLY
RELIEVED and HAPPY.
THANK YOU, THANK YOU, THANK YOU.
Lots of love.
Richard

Call every actor, crew member and agent to relay the great news. Bone-crunchingly hug my poor wife and daughter, who have endured this marathon alongside me so loyally.

The race is now on to get a great first assistant director. As I'm not waiting for the French to come up with someone, I call the shortlist of people I have worked with before and others who come highly recommended.

One of them, Charlie Watson, offers to come over on Sunday to discuss the project.

*Everything* galvanized and firing on ten thousand cylinders.

## 25 April 2004

Charlie Watson is a no-shit-Sherlock testo-charged soldier of a man, who comes with a game plan, is incredibly organized and speaks practical sense about getting everything in shit-shape order *pronto*. Perfect. He has read the script, gets the humour and requires none of the explanations of things that I had to give Valerie, simply because we speak the same language. The relief is huge. Also speaks French. Usually works with second AD Alex Oakley and it is my mission now to get Marie-Castille to agree to employing both these guys. It'll be a huge help having them in London to organize the actors' costume and wig fittings, medicals and the revised shooting schedule.

Can only guess how this idea will go down across the Channel.

## 26 April 2004

Eurostar'd to Paris with Gary Williamson, who has been an absolute tower of support and good humour throughout this chaos. Go to the Loma Nasha office and meet line producer Pascal Ralite, Pierre Aïm and Laurence. Headless-chicken situation – they don't have a possible list of alternative French first assistant directors, haven't got the last schedule made by Valerie, or her notes, and she is now in Australia. In other words, in the six-week hiatus, it appears *no* plans were made to replace Valerie. They try to access the schedule on their computer and it takes Gary phoning his assistant in London to explain to them what to do to get one finally printed out. *The Goon Show* for real.

This is the perfect cue for me to say I had a list of English assistant directors, Charlie Watson being my first choice and immediately available. Marie-Castille arrives an hour late for the meeting and on hearing this suggestion, refuses point blank and walks out of the room. Pascal, who has worked with her before, whispers that this is par for the course and he would speak to her.

Like they have a lot of choice right now! True to his word, half an hour later she comes back in and bemoans the fact that English crew all have agents and ask for too much money compared to the French. I ignored this and tried to make sense of the immediate problem of readjusting the schedule to start shooting on 7 June.

As the first assistant director, whoever he/she might be, has to recce every location and rework the schedule, plans are made to fly to Swaziland as soon as possible.

Marie-Castille, who has calmed down, casually asks for Charlie Watson's agent's number. I ask her about the *Camelot* music rights and she assures me that Valerie Lindon in Paris secured them three weeks ago for thirty per cent less than the London quote. When I ask for Valerie's phone number so that she can cross-collate with Maggie Rodford about playback piano tapes, she claims not to have it! Aha!

Just before we're due to catch our train back, I am summoned to a side room with Pierre Kubel and Marie-Castille, lectured about the budget cuts, the absence of any contingency or financial safety net, and that as producers they are earning *nothing* on the film. *Nothing*. Therefore, in order for the film to proceed, I would have to agree to a fee that is a *quarter* of my contracted figure, *half* of which would be deferred. In my experience, for 'deferred' read '*never ever seen, ever*'. The total fee for writing, directing, practically co-producing, prep, shooting and post-production editing would amount to a pittance. *Plus* I hand over all rights to them.

I nod throughout, knowing that they're doing this without lawyers or agents present, them *knowing* how desperate I am to make the film. I recognize that a line has been crossed. When I counter that she has been in possession of my writer-director's contract for the past two years, she says it was not agreed with her but with the previous producers. Get on the train with Gary, seething, and call my literary agent.

### 27 April 2004

The whole day is taken up by back-and-forth negotiations with Charlie Watson's agent, Jackie. He is being offered about half his going rate, and he says he won't do it. Jackie keeps me fully informed throughout.

They then try to get Charlie's second assistant, Alex Oakley, to be the first AD, again at a lower rate than he usually works for. But at least Pascal is an experienced line producer and had the decency to hear me out yesterday when I outlined how crucial it was to have two English guys doing this job, in the absence of *any* French contenders. He did not disagree, and it is on this basis that I am determined now to stick out for what I need.

### 28 April 2004

Alex and Charlie will not play victim to MC's divide-and-rule tactics and both refuse to do the job without the other. I then offer to make up the shortfall to ensure we get Alex on board, to which his agent agrees. To have two real professionals by my side at this point is worth so much more than the few extra thousand pounds it costs. Chrissie Baker is finally contracted to do hair and make-up.

7.46 p.m. – after endless haggling, both Alex and Charlie are 'on board'.

Having peeked into the trough of insomnia during these past agonizing weeks, the news that these two guys are onside is the best sleeping pill I could have wished for.

Gary Williamson flew to Swaziland this evening. It has truly begun, and nothing is going to stop me now. *Nothing.*

## *29 April 2004*

MC is on the phone going ballistic at me for offering to supplement the shortfall in Alex Oakley's salary, blathering and frothing about how easy it was to get alternative second ADs and why did the English all have agents and how dare I do this as it would cause chaos amongst the crew that these two ADs were getting so excessively well paid and would cause a riot of bad feeling. On and on she goes, cage fully rattled.

When she draws breath, I calmly say, 'I will do *anything* to ensure that my film gets made properly and within the already overloaded and curtailed shooting schedule. Charlie and Alex are my best bet at achieving this as a first-time director, and if there is not enough money to pay them, I am more than happy to make up the shortfall. *Every* film has salary discrepancies, from actors, local and imported, through to crew members both local and imported. This is always the case and in my experience has never caused problems. It is an accepted fact of the industry. And, if Alex does *not* do the film, Charlie won't either.'

I had to repeat this last sentence to her five times before she seemed to finally understand.

I was so calm I unnerved myself. She clearly has no concept that she cannot communicate like most people naturally do.

# DEVELOPMENT

No sooner done than my literary agent issues MC's lawyer an ultimatum about my contract in response to her position that she had not agreed my contract, which she has had for two years. However, in the light of the reduced budget and the saga securing finance, I agree to a compromise, but not the ludicrous fee she and Kubel came up with at the start of the week in Paris.

Gloves off all round now.

Meanwhile, Charlie wastes no time in organizing Karen Jones to come round and do a script read and timing, and is more on the ball than anyone has been so far, easing the considerable load I have borne on my own for too long now. The relief is incalculable.

Went to Mary Selway's beautiful, celebratory funeral at lunchtime, packed with every famous actor, director and writer she had discovered, nurtured and supported throughout her brilliant career.

# PRE-PRODUCTION

## 2 May 2004

Packed all my Pelham puppets, tin toys, flags, old binoculars and cine cameras for the return to Swaziland. Spent the day with my wife and daughter doing 'normal' things again – walking the dog along the river, buying ice creams, chatting and trying to get our heads around the fact that this time tomorrow I will be at the bottom of Africa in another hemisphere. Try as I might, I can't settle and am itching to get on the plane.

Meet Charlie at the airport and immediately address the schedule breakdown – him having to catch up in no time at all what took the former AD some time to arrive at, simply due to English not being her first language. The script is broken down into numbers of people, props, extras needed and timing of each scene. We establish our modus operandi of blocking the scene first thing in the morning with the actors, before the lighting, costume, hair and make-up work starts, and aim to roll cameras by 8.30 as winter daylight hours are short – it's dark by 5.30 p.m. Charlie suggests running buffet lunches on the days when we have especially large numbers of scenes and cast to deal with, to avoid the post-lunch torpor that so often slows everything down. His experience is hugely reassuring and all this practical talk eases away any nerves I have. At midnight, a British Airways hostess whispers that there is a spare flat bed in first class if I want it. I go to sleep peacefully, thinking about the thrill of getting my first Aiwa cassette recorder in 1969, way before the advent of CDs, DVDs, iPods and email.

# THE WAH-WAH DIARIES

## 3 May 2004

Five-hour minibus drive to Swaziland from Jo'burg. Arrive at Boshimela, perched on top of a mountain with an incredible sweeping view of the valley below. Jane Stephens lives in a house on the estate, and after her parents died last year in their nineties, the family took the decision to leave everything intact and untouched. It is a house with a history, furniture, books, cutlery and crockery all circa 1965. Already a virtual film set, it is the answer to my dream visual requirements, and is also isolated from traffic noise, aeroplanes or outside intrusions, making it the perfect location to record sound. Gary Williamson is waiting for us and we both get pretty emotional that we are *finally* here and starting proper.

However, Jane needs a lot of reassurance regarding the size of the operation ahead. Where will the crew be fed? Where will the actors' caravans be placed? Where will the lighting and catering trucks be parked? How many people will be working at any given time, what security will be in place, what time will we start work, how much prep time is needed and how long will it take to clear up once filming is completed?

How do you explain to someone who has never been near a film set before that nothing short of a mini-invasion is ahead? That a hundred and twenty people will take over every inch of space, start work before dawn and leave after dark, store equipment, cables and lighting gear, erect a marquee to feed this army, install lamps and scaffolding inside every room, move furniture and inhabit a family's most private domain in the most public way possible?

I feel like Kofi Annan trying to offer reassurance and promises that I doubt I can practically keep. *Nothing* can prepare a house owner for the onslaught of people required to make a film. I opt for the tactic of asking Jane where, what and how she thinks it best to accommodate the masses, and am thrilled by her offer that we use an open field at the back of the property to house the catering marquee and the actor, make-up and costume caravans, a nearby paddock to park the electric generator and lighting trucks, and a guest cottage beside the main house to store the props and furniture brought in by the art department.

The recce plan is to follow the shooting schedule that essentially starts in the north of Swaziland and ends in the far south – in a mere three days! Charlie follows Pierre Aïm, Gary and me as we plot through every single scene in the film, taking copious notes and making floor plans of camera tracks and suchlike. Professional and methodical.

What a relief to be dealing with the practicals of shooting rather than all the horse shit of the past weeks. I just hope Jane does not have a thrombosis when she finally sees the arrival of trucks, cars, caravans and troops in a few weeks' time. Likewise, I hope I don't have a seizure trying to rally everything into the tight shooting schedule ahead. One day at a time . . .

### 4 May 2004

Spend three days charging from one location to the next, all the while placating and reassuring each local person we meet that the film is in fact going to happen. As this is the third time they have heard this spiel from me in as many years, they can be forgiven for looking sceptical.

Zoe Dean-Smith, with whom I was at school, suggests I meet Mathokoza Sibiyu, a Swazi computer programmer and amateur-choir conductor at the Theatre Club for the role of Dozen. When I mention that his character requires a sense of humour to enable him to get 'whited up' to play Lancelot in *Camelot*, he is already laughing and I am grinning and thrilled that he is the right man for the role. He sings like a dream, and though he has no acting experience whatsoever, his immediate charm and openness convince me that he is a risk worth taking. Significantly, his peripatetic job means that he is not deskbound and can fit in with the inevitable vagaries of a changing shooting schedule.

Relief that I don't have to import an actor from South Africa.

### 5 May 2004

My forty-seventh birthday. Woke at 5 a.m. With the sun just up I sat in my hotel bed full of circular thoughts about having been born here and now returned to shoot my own life, the out-of-body experience of examining locations where the events actually took place and trying objectively to assess the practicalities of parking, access, permissions, proximity to other locations in the schedule and so on. And everywhere the ghosts of my past, anecdotes and stories silently competing with Charlie Watson's queries about where, what and how, with Pierre Aïm the cinematographer asking for details about how I want the scenes set up and shot.

Having thought I wouldn't know the answers to anything, I am motor-mouthing in all directions without a moment's doubt. Exhilarated.

### 6 May 2004

Gary Williamson and set decorator Flo Ballack spend three hours in the back of the equatorially hot minivan meticulously trawling through every prop in the script, asking detailed questions as we drive along the roughest dirt road imaginable from the south of the country up north back to Pigg's Peak. Bizarre to be explaining a watermelon 'porcupine' for a party scene – halved melon covered with toothpicks, loaded up with cubed cheese and chemically coloured cocktail onions.

A.D. Van Wyk, the local transport mogul with a private collection of Mercedes-Benzes stored in a warehouse, is the answer to every dream car requirement in the script. His collection is the life-size version of my Dinky toy collection from the sixties and none of us can believe our luck. A.D. enthusiastically says we can hire whatever we want – and there is a lot to want, including the perfect ruby-red 1968 sports car for Ruby. Must double-check whether Emily Watson can drive . . . Station wagons, motorbikes, jeeps, a Morris Minor and a cream coloured, leather-upholstered 1967 Benz for the hero, complete the wish list. A.D. also offers to be on hand for filming and to have a mechanic on set every day. Pierre asks whether it's possible to remove the back seats and doors to get the camera installed, which could have had A.D. showing us the door, but he doesn't!

I'm struck by the absence of suspicion and dollar signs in his dealings, reminding me that small-town values are not entirely a thing of the past; the compliant generosity he displays is something I remember from my childhood. This is reiterated when we drop in on Dr John and Glenda Stephens, who allow Gary and me to scour their house for potential props and furniture. Dr John is brother of Jane, part-owner of Boshimela, whilst Glenda I have known since I was four. She is the one remaining person in Swaziland who knew all the same characters I did who feature in the script. The two of them talk about the Aids pandemic, people from the past, snake bites, fruit-stealing monkeys, the odd foiled burglary and someone who blasted her adulterous husband with a shotgun, and in the weave and weft of their conversation I am again reminded that life south of the Equator is very different to London. There is a benign, amused acceptance that life is lived here outside the rulebooks of Western living. The more we talk, the more I realize that there is an odd comfort in accepting living on the brink and edge of chaos. Which is essentially the nature of filming.

Glenda's son, Mark, has just graduated from Cape Town Drama School and agreed to work as an art-department runner and extra in the *Camelot* scenes.

Get word that Gregor Telfer, the great props master from *Gosford Park*, has taken a big-budget film, so I have another crew member to find. The hunt is also on to find a working sixties radiogram . . .

### 7 May 2004

Five-hour minibus schlep across relentlessly bleak flat landscape to Jo'burg in contrast to the mountain beauty of Swaz. The urban sprawl is characterized by high walls, topped off with electrified razor wire and signs promising 'ARMED RESPONSE'. We visit costume-rental companies stuffed with fifties and early sixties floral clothes that give us good reason to call Sheena Napier, the designer, with confirmation that there is local stock available. She is climbing walls in London as the actors' contracts have yet to be confirmed, and with four weeks to go before shooting, Sheena is up against it – the protocol being that actors cannot be contacted for measurements and fittings *until* their contracts have been settled. I tell her to go ahead anyway.

Leave Charlie in the hotel to wrangle with the schedule cuts and bomb off with Gary to some second-hand stores in search of a radiogram. Half an hour later we are shown a 1959 Blaupunkt in perfect working order which has a Nat King Cole record on it. I'm not super-stitious, but this is sweet serendipity as his recording of 'Stay As Sweet As You Are' is central to a crucial reunion scene halfway through the film. The dealer embarks on some heavy-duty air-sucking through his dentures, deciding just how much to fleece us. He cautiously looks up from beneath his Brylcreemed quiff, clearly unchanged since he was eighteen in 1948, and says, '480 rand?'– £48. I attempt to demur and he inhales some *Antiques Roadshow* propriety, like he's presiding over a Bechstein grand. I concur, Gary is already unscrewing the legs and we haul our loot into the back of the van. Gary informs me that this is the first time he has had a director buying his own props.

### 8 May 2004

9 a.m. call at the house of Christa Schamberger, the Jo'burg casting director, to videotape actors for supporting parts. John Matshikiza, who'd lived in exile in London during the Apartheid era, Michael Richard, Ian Roberts and Michelle Maxwell, all of whom I knew in the late seventies, and all of whom play leading roles in South Africa, generously agree to play small parts in *Wah-Wah*.

I meet Clare Marshall, a Liz Taylor look-alike whom I had seen in *Gypsy* thirty-two years ago and remembered her sassy presence. She's perfect for the cameo role of the box-office manageress.

Have to quell feelings of fraudulence playing the part of film director, having never shot a frame as yet, but I love the avalanche of questions and decisions about any and everything that is becoming the daily norm.

Each actor has date-juggling problems and I hope that they can all be accommodated.

## 9 May 2004

Back to London and my wife and daughter have organized a surprise birthday dinner with my favourite friends and food, which is the perfect post-location-recce-lagged homecoming a man could wish for.

## 10 May 2004

Email Laurence at Loma Nasha requesting that I meet potential French editors ASAP to avoid the last-minute-panic syndrome, on the grounds that the editor is the most crucial crew member to secure, and the person with whom I will spend more time than anyone else.

Speak at length with a French director who has worked with MC and he feels that she thrives on conflict. I'm relieved it's not just me, but something that she does with others. He kindly gives me a list of possible French editors' names and their phone numbers.

## 11 May 2004

MC calls Charlie Watson and demands that he make *further* cuts to the shooting schedule with the proviso 'not to tell Richard'. Charlie is on the blower immediately and we both wonder at how she thinks cuts can be made *without* my knowledge!!

First rehearsal – American accent session with my wife, Joan Washington, and Emily Watson. Joan has generously agreed to coach Emily and Nicholas Hoult for free, as there is no budget provision made for this. This is the first time I have ever worked with my wife in coach/director mode.

I'm very nervous as I hold Emily in such great esteem, and don't want to make a complete plonker of myself. She dives straight in, doing the accent and asking detailed questions about her role, with such concentrated focus that all nerves are bypassed instantly. It's an incredible privilege to work with an actor whose talent has that instant alchemical ability to transform words on a page into a three-dimensional person. Having heard the words for so long in my head, there is a palpable thrill to hear her bring them to life with such innate understanding. She takes everything at her own measured pace, never allowing anything to be generalized, staying true to her instincts and constantly searching for that intangible something which makes a character live. Compassionate, innately warm and sympathetic – these are the qualities Emily naturally exudes, all of which make her 'reading' of Ruby so instantly powerful. *This* is what makes the process so exhilarating and worthwhile, amidst all the producer nonsense.

Emily is concerned that she is playing the only American character in a cast of British actors, and asks that Joan always be available for coaching.

*12 May 2004*

Went ballistic upon discovering, by chance, that MC has produced a promotional poster for the film market in Cannes without consulting me or extending the basic courtesy of letting me see it first, claiming that it was all done at the last minute. The clichéd image is *everything* I want to avoid for a film set in Africa – a white-safari-suited nine-year-old boy, book in hand, flanked by African warriors and a fucking tame lion, looking into the distance. When I vent my stupefaction at this, I am rewarded with a character-assassination email from her. My reply –

Dear Marie-Castille,

I received your email this evening, the *fifth* I have received since 18 March, eight weeks ago . . .

My frustration has been entirely to do with the continuous lack of communication from you, the most recent being the Cannes poster. You only respond quickly when you have something to criticise – your latest email accusing me of having an 'obsession to always find the negative in everything and despise the positive and good'.

If this was true, I doubt I would have attracted the calibre of actors and crew that I have done. You need only ask Martin Jaubert, Pascal Ralite, Charlie, Lynne-Anne and Gary how incredibly successful and positive the recent recce to Swaziland went, in which I, along with everyone else, did our utmost to *positively* reassure people about locations and use of their property and get to grips with the tight schedule.

I may not have directed a film before, but have worked as an actor on over thirty with some of the best writers, directors and crews around. It is the director who steers the film and this is what I am in the process of doing.

I am writing this to clear the air and to establish a proper professional working relationship with you. This is not *beyond your control*, as you claim. It is *entirely within your control*. It's simply called communicating – in order to collaborate and make the best film we possibly can.

I am in constant daily contact with Gary in Swaziland, Lynne-Anne in Cape Town and Charlie Watson in London – all of whom channel everything through Martin Jaubert in Paris. This has proved to be incredibly positive, fruitful and professional. It is open and trusting.

As you claim to *celebrate the positive*, why not try to communicate some of this to your director and crew?

As I have said to you before, I am deeply grateful to you for negotiating and securing the excellent cast and crew we now have on the film. I invite you to the read-through at my house on Monday, 24 May, at 10.30am, if you can make it . . .

Yours,

Richard

A collision course is set and I must do all I can to avoid it. I dread the knock-on effect it will have in the months ahead.

Divert myself making individual music CDs for each actor according to what their character would have listened to.

### *14 May 2004*

Eurostar to Paris to meet editors – having been told ad nauseam by MC that it is not necessary to secure an editor in advance of the shoot and that they should only start editing *after* the shooting is completed. Have to go through the pantomime of telling her that having spoken to five directors, I *have* to get an editor up front so that we have a rough assembly of the film within a week of completing the shooting. Yet again, this seemingly perfectly normal working practice is met with frustrating resistance. Having finally agreed to find a requisite French editor, the choice is limited as it has been left so late and people are booked months in advance. Her line producer, Pascal, is keen that I meet his friend Luc Barnier. However, I have previously got a list of the best editors from Antoine de Caunes, who has put me in touch with the doyenne of French editors, who in turn strongly recommends that I try and meet Isabelle Dedieu. I refused to meet two of MC's suggestions, as both of them had unheard of credits and precious little experience. One claimed to have worked with Altman, so I called Bob and he had no memory of her whatsoever. When I relayed this back, it was met with the usual non-response.

Gary calls at dawn from Swaziland to report that there is still no production office set up or even a phone line, because the cash has not been cleared. Meanwhile Charlie Watson is fighting to get cash to pay for the wigs and costume rentals, because the dealers in which won't release their gear until they are sure of payment. With only three weeks to go before shooting, it is surely not an unreasonable request.

Meet Isabelle Dedieu, who it turns out has not even been sent a script, so I find myself having to pitch the story to her cold during her rushed lunch hour – the surest indication that the producers want me to go with *their* choice of editor. We instantly connect and I like her enormously, plus her English is as fluent as my French is crippled.

First time I have seen MC face to face since her critical email, and I resolve to put on a show of benign charm. I request that Isabelle be sent a script, and then endure the discomfort of being driven across Paris in MC's Smart-car to meet editor Luc Barnier, who – surprise surprise – *has* been sent the script in advance of our meeting.

Within five nanoseconds she is firing on all cylinders.

'You have to cut two more days out of the schedule. And *all* the actors' deals are exceeding the budget quote.'

'What do you suggest cutting?'

She could not think of anything but insisted that it had to be cut. Then she dropped her second bomb. 'I have to go to Cannes tomorrow to meet the co-producers as *nothing* has been signed yet. Everything is in total chaos.'

I kept smiling, kept supernaturally calm and retorted that everything was going perfectly well at my end.

Not another word. I knew her cage was well and truly rattled, contrary to her claims that she was utterly without fear and full of positivity. I manage a cheery 'bon chance'.

So much for producer 'reassurance'.

Luc is charm itself but, crucially, is unavailable until September. Isabelle has already won me over with her conviction that *anyone* can shoot, act, design and edit with a degree of competence, but the chief failure of most films is a lack of personal viewpoint and vision. This is what sets a great movie apart. Everything else is 'window dressing'. Everything about her attitude was reassuring, nurturing, empathetic, collaborative and, even though we only met for half an hour, I felt sure that if she responded to the script, we could work well together. A crucial decision, as we will be locked away together in an edit room for months.

### 15 May 2004

Scoured Portobello Market for a stall selling Super 8 cine cameras. Bought a box of cheap broken cameras and found a dozen pairs of old binoculars as props for the Independence celebrations sequence.

Call from Isabelle, who enthused for half an hour about the script – she 'gets' everything and feels committed and passionate about editing it. Called MC immediately and having no alternative, she reluctantly agreed to my choice. Huge relief to have *finally* secured the technical triumvirate I need to make the film: cinematographer, editor and first assistant director. *Ecstatic!*

### 16 May 2004

Charlie Watson comes round at 9 a.m. to shave two days off the schedule. It takes us the best part of the day to cut *one* day. Call Gary in Swaz and ask if he will go and look at an alternative mission-school location in order to lose the second day. Still no production phone line, meaning that calls are at international mobile rates. Insane.

Sheena Napier calls asking for the Swazi cast members' costume measurements ASAP. This pattern of yo-yoing between the 'bigger picture' and minutiae of centimetre measurements and suchlike is now a constant.

### 17 May 2004

Charlie and Alex Oakley bowl in for a second day of schedule shaving. Alex is a man of persistent good humour, piercing blue eyes and a boyish 'fuck 'em all' charm that is perfect for corralling actors onto the set, overseeing the daily work call sheet and keeping the backstage wheels from falling off.

Evening at Air-Edel sound studios recording the piano playback of all the *Camelot* songs featured in the film, organized by composer Pat Doyle and his manager and music publisher, Maggie Rodford. Again, their complete professionalism is reassuring and inspiring – everything is possible and nothing too much trouble.

### 18 May 2004

Rehearsal with a very jet-lagged Nicholas Hoult, just back from Chicago where he has completed filming *The Weather Man*. He's a worrying *four inches* taller than when he first auditioned in November. Which means he will tower over Gabriel Byrne.

He and Emily connect immediately and it is exhilarating, even at this initial stage, to see them work together so easily. Afterwards Emily says, 'He's just got it.' And what that is, is total focus and emotional openness that belies his fourteen years. He doesn't strike a false note and makes it all seem as natural and effortless as you could wish for. Lucky, lucky me.

### 19 May 2004

D-Day – completely panic-stricken call from MC, who is in Cannes, *begging* me to call the government office at the Department of Culture, Media and Sport (DCMS) dealing with the *Wah-Wah* co-production application, which *should* have been filed four weeks *prior* to start of shooting, pleading for clemency. I have to haul my already dumbstruck jaw from the floor. The DCMS in London requires a strict breakdown of the British cast and crew paying tax to qualify as a co-production. If the budget percentages are not met, the application will be refused. No application, no film. I can't believe this has not already been dealt with, whatever the reasons.

I phone Scion's Jeff Abberley immediately – 'Why didn't you call me about this a month ago?'

He claims that MC advised him not to bother me with all this as I was too busy and that she and I had such a *close* relationship, everything should go via her, as we were 'at one'!! Ye olde divide-and-rule tactics????

MC gives me the name of the DCMS man from whom I have to *beg* a stay of execution. His opening gambit: 'You've broken the law and cannot start shooting on 7 June.' Emphatic and unyielding.

I've only ever had a few parking fines, so I'm not really prepared for this. I explain as humbly and best I can that due to the stop-start, up-down-and-sideways nature of raising money, and what with the recent change in the film-finance tax laws that saw upwards of thirty films collapse overnight, our start date has been so messed about that our application has passed the minimum four-week deadline. I follow up with a detailed email about being locked into location and actor availability in Swaziland, all of which collapse if we start any later.

This is something I should not be dealing with. After some truly gruesome grovelling, he grudgingly agrees to reconsider and will get back to me. He calls later to advise that the completed application *must* be emailed to his office by 9 a.m. tomorrow. His exasperated tone leaves me feeling like a five-year-old getting bollocked by a very justifiably disgruntled headmaster.

MC's sidekick calls to ask me to phone casting director Celestia Fox to delay the actors by yet another week. Celestia refuses, saying that we will simply lose the main cast if we do so at this late stage.

Gabriel Byrne's agent calls from Dublin saying that she has no deal memo, contract *or* promised money in escrow to guarantee that her client will get paid, and does not get any reply from the French production office despite leaving a plethora of messages. Utter fucking chaos.

Reel around the house trying not to lose my head, reassuring everyone who calls that the film is actually going ahead as planned, knowing that it could all collapse in twenty-four hours. I'm sickened at having to do this, and some acting is required to answer actors' queries about their characters and costumes knowing all this is going on unbeknownst to them.

Lyndsey Posner, lawyer at my agency ICM, calls to reassure me that the fact the DCMS have not turned us down outright is a sign that we might be saved. A much appreciated sliver of hope.

### 20 May 2004

MC calls at 9.30 a.m. in a state of euphoria, like an overexcited teenager – '*we've been up all night, we've been up all night*' to complete the application which was emailed at 7.45 a.m.

## PRE-PRODUCTION

Scion has mercifully appointed Chris Curling from Zephyr Films to be a co-producer who will go between all English and French business. As he has a lot of co-production experience, he will be a hands-on monitor to steer the production out of some of the difficulties it has faced and may face in the future.

### 21 May 2004

House invaded. Alex Oakley has set up office in the kitchen, Miranda Richardson is having a costume fitting in our bedroom with Sheena Napier and her assistant Tamar Zaig, Fenella Woolgar is having a wig fitting in the bathroom with Chrissie Baker, and I am meeting Julian Wadham to discuss the script. Each room issues a pile of questions that require answers, everything from 'How much mosquito repellent will we need?' to 'What is the subtext of this particular phrase?' and 'Is this hem the right length?' Spent valuable rehearsal time with Fenella and Julian charting the arc of their characters' subplot romance, clarifying their 'status' in the strict colonial pecking order, filling them in with as much character detail as they need. *This* is what I am supposed to be doing and it goes a long way to alleviate the stress of worrying about production issues.

No sooner do I feel this than Alex moseys in and says he has had word from Swaziland that the government require medical certificates along with every crew and cast member's work-permit application, along with proof that no one has been in prison. Well, how the fuck do you do that with no time to go? Oh, and all the prop cigarettes which are herbal/non-tobacco for use in the film have been confiscated at the airport in Jo'burg en route to Swaziland. Oh, oh, *and* no money has yet been released in time to secure a local production office or get the phone line connected, so they are still using mobiles and Gary Williamson's hotel room as an office. Morale is low and Alex suggests I call to try and gee them all up.

Relief that, despite all the problems, Gabriel Byrne is now confirmed and will arrive in London on 30 May for costume fittings and make-up tests before leaving for Swaziland on 4 June. Only when faced with the reality that he will bail out unless officially contracted does MC manage to move her arse in the nick of.

### 22 May 2004

Wander through Portobello hunting for more last-minute props, wondering whether I will actually be flying to Swaziland next week or not.

Call from Alex to say that Martin Jaubert, the French production manager, is in hospital in Paris having contracted some unidentified tropical disease from the last location recce and might not be able to do the film. What else can go wrong at this stage?

Shopped for food for the read-through the day after tomorrow, which my wife has generously agreed to co-host and co-cook with me. Did further rewrites to accommodate the shortened schedule, collated all the background photos, music and props.

### 24 May 2004

Perfect sunny weather for the cast and English crew read-through in our kitchen. Without Gabriel Byrne or Celia Imrie – she is on 'Bridget Jones 2' duty. Gruesome actor nerves all round. Julie Walters is an hour late, having got the start time muddled up, giving everyone else a chance to ease in together. Such is Julie's instant comic impact on arrival that we finally start in the best possible humour.

It's the first time I have heard my script read out loud all the way through and am truly thrilled when people laugh and even more surprised when they are clearly moved by the end.

Everyone clapped and the excitement about all going to Africa together feels like we're about to go on an Enid Blyton adventure. Cross-cut with the Kafkaesque possibility that it could all go belly up. But have to believe that Julie's four-year commitment to and faith in this film *has* to count for something and we *will* get it made!

Everyone is stuffing their faces and downing champagne and as gung-ho and ready to roll as you could possibly wish for. Miranda asks about mosquitoes and if you can get Aids from being bitten. Never considered this and promise to check it out, whilst reassuring everyone that having never heard of this, it seems unlikely. Plus the fact that we are shooting in the middle of winter when there are none around.

MC calls in the evening to ask if I've heard from the DCMS yet.

### 25 May 2004

Woken at dawn by the dog going berserk, and discover that a fox has just eaten the nine ducklings that have recently hatched in the garden.

Receive an email confirming that the late DCMS application will in principle be approved with the proviso that all their conditions are adhered to and that we *can* start shooting on 7 June!

I call MC with this great news and her response is to slag off the British government for 'taking so long'. Called Scion who are hugely relieved, although they are still waiting for the budget break-down, promised to them by her . . . Meanwhile the props buyer in Jo'burg is putting all her costs onto her personal credit card. The fact that the good faith of the crew is liable to this kind of abuse is head-imploding.

Call MC's producing partner, Pierre, about getting the *Clockwork Orange* poster which he has promised to provide for the art department and which I am due to take with me when I leave for Swaziland. Comes as 'news' to him when I mention the start date. He heads a film-poster company in Paris which re-jigs American poster campaigns for the French market, and says he has a copy.

'In English?' I ask.

The moment's silence is long enough to tell me that it's not, and with a day to go before I fly out for the shoot, he suggests *I* track one down in London.

Distracted off to Pinewood Studios to do a voice recording for Tim Burton's animated *Corpse Bride* and am instantly struck by the obvious camaraderie and team spirit between director and producers . . .

Get home to agent mayhem. MC hasn't provided Gabriel's agent, Teri Hayden, with a promised bank letter about the escrow agreement, but said to her that all the other lead actors had agreed to a deferment of the last third of their salaries till the end of November. Teri is annoyed and all the agents have demanded that the deal memos be adhered to or their clients won't show up. It is a measure of their collective forbearance and faith in the project that they have not told us all to take a hike.

Conference call from Chris Curling and Scion confirming that the film is fully financed, but that the cash flow will be delayed till next week. They hadn't heard that Pascal is no longer line-producing as he has had to withdraw due to his wife's illness. Martin Jaubert is also not allowed to leave Paris for another week due to his condition, so we will start shooting without *any* producer out there, at the time they are most needed to get everything running smoothly. It'll be up to South African Lynne-Anne to take up the slack. She calls to say that the South African co-producers have not yet paid the transport company delivering the props and furniture to Swaziland, so they are awaiting payment in Jo'burg, three hundred miles away. Gary is understandably having a thrombosis as it will be his neck on the line if the sets are not ready and dressed on the 7th.

Oh, and the hotel manager is bleating for his deposit on the hundred rooms booked for the five-week shoot in Pigg's Peak and says unless he is paid, he will have to let them go. MC's standard response is 'the money will be there *tomorrow*'.

Agree to keep Scion informed on a daily basis by phone and email of how things are progressing, and they try to reassure me that they will do all they can to help put out the endless fires that seem to be igniting all over the place.

Found one desperate duckling down a hole, got it out and within minutes its mum had flown in, but held out little hope it would survive the night. Having hoped for a couple of hours' respite with my family before flying to Africa, am now thoroughly wired and stressed out by the mess of it all. Night flight to Jo'burg taken up with further schedule shuffling.

I dare to hope that things might begin to run more smoothly in the days ahead.

### 27 May 2004

Today would have been my dad's seventy-sixth birthday, and I'm on my way to recreate his life and death where it actually all took place, twenty-six years ago. On the minivan journey from Jo'burg to Swaz, Pierre the cinematographer worries out loud about getting the correct film stock out of Jo'burg in time, then gets a phone call from MC who tells him that she feels she deserves a medal for getting the film on its feet!

Five-hour schlep to the border, after which spirits revive once in Swaziland, driving through the stunning mountains again towards Pigg's Peak.

Cannot *quite* believe this is *it*, but reality noses in fast when Charlie Watson appears grim-faced and reports that morale is very low, there is still no cash flow, and – worst of all – despite my bleating for the past two years to MC to get work permits sorted, and despite being told by MC *not* to concern myself with these production details, the reality is that we *don't* have permits for the cast or crew. I am not sure who is at fault but a distraught Lynne-Anne reports that there is now a fifteen-strong government committee to deal with who have not been informed about the filming. It appears there has been no adequate follow-up since our last location recce.

I'm so genuinely relieved to be here and finally starting, that clearly the only way forward is to get to grips with the logistics and staging requirements of each scene with Charlie, Pierre and Gary. Relative calm prevails for four intense hours with Charlie keeping detailed notes. Problem-solving is something Charlie revels in and I feel absolutely certain he will ensure that things run smoothly.

Conference call with *all* the producers and co-producers on line together for the first time and I am stupefied to hear MC drumming up compliments for herself in the stony absence of any being offered, verbally stroking herself for how hard she has worked. When I inform her about the work-permit fuck-up, she nonchalantly exhorts me to 'go and shmooze the Swazi government'. Like I don't have enough to do already.

When I ask *who* precisely she dealt with when she was last out here, and to email me her paperwork, she says, 'Oh, that fat old Swazi guy,' and 'No, I don't have any paperwork.' I suppose the only 'consolation' is that a dozen other people are witness to this quite staggering response. She tops it off by declaring that she can't wait to get out here and 'produce'. Charlie and Gary shake their heads in utter *disbelief*.

Better news is that the props truck has made it through the night to the border, and is only a couple of hours away. And then there is the winter night sky – a dome of stars, so clear, so vast and so awe-inspiring, that *none* of this shite is going to stop me having the time of my life, realizing something I have dreamt of doing for over twenty years. Even though I have lived in England as long as I ever lived in Swaz, I feel completely at home. The sounds and night-time smell of it all is so familiar-foreign and nostalgic that I count myself a very lucky boy to be back again.

Slept deeply.

### 28 May 2004

7 a.m. run in the surrounding hills behind the hotel, and not a human in sight. 8 a.m., continue blocking the remainder of the scenes at Boshimela. Feel completely clear about what I want/need to see/feel. Pierre and I are in total tandem about the whys, hows and wherefores.

In the afternoon we rushed into nearby Pigg's Peak, a dusty village with basic food stores, a petrol station and people milling about listlessly, to locate a man with a Polaroid camera to get photos for our work-permit applications. We spot his tripod outside a shop and ask inside after its owner; someone thinks he could be somewhere across the road and might not be back for a while. While we sit and wait, the insanity of schedules, contracts and the million other details of pre-production suddenly becomes clear. Beyond our control! The photographer returns and snap, snap, snap he makes three white men's faces light up, this being the first stage in securing our elusive work permits.

## 29 May 2004

Ninety-minute drive to the capital, Mbabane, and into a neighbouring valley to see Gary's alternative mission-school location. Perfect, unchanged since it was built in the fifties. Reconfigure the script so that an interior classroom scene can be done outdoors beneath a vast acacia tree. Once we have clarified where we will lay camera tracks, checked every angle through a viewfinder and parked all the technical vehicles, we scramble into town to the Theatre Club, which is in a state of real decrepitude since its heyday when the English expat community frequented it. Most of the lighting and sound equipment has been stolen or broken and the club has dwindled into a desultory drinking den with a total of fifty members. This former social hub, a mere husk.

Work out that we will need twenty camera/lighting set-ups per day to complete all the scenes of *Camelot* here in four days. This is impossible as we will have upwards of a hundred extras as well as all of the cast. Much head shaking and rumblings all round. Hunker down with Charlie and, after some shifting back and forth, he claws an extra half-day out of the end of the week by expertly reshuffling scenes. I am determined not to lose these theatre scenes, despite the endless call for cuts from MC, as they are the antidote to the drunken domestic scenes and focus of the expat society in the story.

Gary says he is happy for Tom Bayly, a local architect who directed the original production of *Camelot* in the seventies, to come on board to help with the decor design. He puts me in touch with a woman whose horse we can hire for half a day's filming.

Lynne-Anne calls to say that having read the script, the government committee are concerned about the swearing and the image of Swaziland the film will give. Given the Aids pandemic, this hardly registers on my scale.

## 30 May 2004

Dawn run clears my head and guarantees forty minutes every day where I can't be asked anything. Despite generous offers to stay with old friends, it is not practical as I am here to work and I have to tread diplomatically so as not to seem ungrateful. Instead we're staying at the Royal Swazi Hotel in the Ezulweni Valley, which is set in beautiful grounds and gardens.

The search is on for a suitable cinema venue – both the drive-in and the old cinema were shut down twenty years ago with the arrival of television – and we discover that the hotel has a convention centre with a lighting box and raked seating that will work perfectly for the scene where the two teenagers watch the forbidden *Clockwork Orange*.

Charlie asks for the afternoon alone to work on yet another schedule revision. Gary and Pierre go the health spa for a massage. I drive up into Mbabane and visit my father's grave. What was formerly a giant tree-colonnaded sanctuary of manicured graves is now bleak, overgrown and thoroughly neglected, marked by tree stumps, collapsed tombstones and the realization that the living descendants of those buried here have all long since left the country. The sweeping view down the Ezulweni Valley is as staggering as ever, and it is somehow oddly right and comforting to see that nature has reclaimed this ground. It took a while to find my father's black granite gravestone, hidden by dense undergrowth and thorn scrub which I cleared away. I lay down on the sun-warmed slab and looked up and back to the time when he was buried in such bizarre circumstances, with the young Swazi priest jumping into his grave, unscrewing the coffin and madly attempting to raise him from the dead. All of which will be recreated up at the Pigg's Peak location in a few weeks' time.

Felt very calm lying above my father's bones, accepting that his life was lived in another century. I'd wondered before I got there whether I was somehow expecting 'something' to happen – which is daft as I am not religious or superstitious – but just felt completely at peace.

Spent the rest of the afternoon 'ghosting' through places from my childhood like Rip Van Winkle, remembering how they were then and seeing how they are now – without exception dilapidated and decrepit. I walked through a deserted St Mark's School, where I had been by turns so abjectly unhappy, but also first kissed, was chosen for a school play, won swimming prizes and acquired lifelong friends and long-forgotten enemies and knee injuries. Peering into the science-room windows at the unchanged high tables, ancient Bunsen burners and old blackboard, I recalled the regular humiliations for describing the colours of chemical reactions in florid detail rather than the H3+2gobbledyO-square-pied-root of it all. I got nine per cent for my mock 'O' level, which unleashed a torrent of 'You'll never survive adulthood' threats from an understandably exasperated Mr Taylor, the science master.

The swimming pool was empty and overgrown and I felt like a five-hundred-year-old man revisiting the planet of his youth. Every house I passed conjured up names, faces and incidents I have not seen or heard about in thirty years, yet *nothing* can undo the magic of being back here again.

The popular wisdom that you can never go back in time is being turned on its head. I *am* back and such is the weird alchemy of art that memory is being reanimated and fictionalized to become its own 'truth'. With a little help from a hundred near-strangers and a ton of equipment and film stock . . .

Returned to the hotel and played tennis with Charlie, followed by dinner with Gary and Pierre, all of whom believe in 'something out there larger than all of us'. Try as I might, my faith resolutely remains earthbound with Darwin.

A man on Swazi TV making a speech is upstaged with a subtitle which reads: 'We apologise for the poor sound quality. This is due to our aged sound equipment.'

## 31 May 2004

Woke at 5 a.m., 6 a.m. and 7 a.m. in increasing heart-thumping anxiety about permits, equipment arriving in time and whether I can keep my nerve. Went for a run pronto!

A week before we start shooting and the production office *finally* has a phone line. All-round gratitude for small mercies.

Magriet calls to warn us that Who Dares Wins – her horse – won't go anywhere near bright lights or be persuaded onto the Theatre Club stage as planned, saying it's best we tether the nag at the door of the backstage area instead. Mini re-write required.

Still no cash flow and Ashleigh Tobias the props buyer is in tears wondering if she will ever get reimbursed. I try to reach *anyone* in the French production office, but only get answer machines. Finally call Chris Curling in London and he manages to get hold of Joel Phiri, the co-producer at IMG in Jo'burg, who agrees to bike cash over to Ashleigh immediately. When Charlie and Gary eventually get through to MC, she is unhappy that Chris Curling was called and says she has not looked at Charlie's three-day-old email of the revised schedule 'because it's a public holiday in France'!

Spent the afternoon casting small roles, including Tony Hatton, my old history master and sometime amateur actor, to play my old primary school teacher.

'What shall I wear?'

'Exactly what you're dressed in now.'

'But there are elbow holes in my cardy.'

'Perfect!'

He is in his late seventies and worried about remembering his lines. His much younger Swazi wife Zanelle is very enthusiastic about being a chorus member in *Camelot*. Ex-pat Helen Donaldson from Dundee, and lifelong friend, agrees to loan ten of her little ballerinas to be part of the film. Despite living in Swaziland for forty years, her Scottish accent is as thick as the day she arrived. Unlike the relatively quick in-and-out nature of professional casting, each meeting is crammed with stories and anecdotes, hospitality, cake and questions, all of which take up time pleasurably, a welcome respite from the tail-chasing demands of everything else.

Alex Oakley arrives from London, Alan Raad, third assistant director, comes in from Jo'burg and Yves Kohen, the electrical 'best boy', lands from Paris, which serves to convince the troops on the ground that it is all starting to move.

I hold an evening meeting in my room with Charlie, Alex and Alan to answer a barrage of questions and delegate what we are all going to be doing in the days and weeks ahead, as well as asking for a list of every cast and crew member's birthday and name-tags for everyone as it's impossible to remember a hundred new names in the first few days of shooting. Alex is the perfect foil for Charlie's no-nonsense approach, and has an infectious insouciance that basically takes the pish out of anything pompous or pretentious. He is flagrantly politically incorrect and already ribbing and teasing French, South African, Swazi and English sensibilities.

Gary calls mid-meeting at 7 p.m. to say that Ashleigh the props buyer has only been given *half* the cash owed her and fobbed off with some bullshit about the full amount being 'misunderstood'. There are questions all round as to whether *some* on the producing end have any idea how frustrating and crippling the lack of cash flow and support is, especially as we have been assured that the film is fully financed.

# PRE-PRODUCTION

## 1 June 2004

Celestia Fox calls to confirm that the promised bank letter to secure Emily Watson has not been received and that Emily will not fly until she has it.

The government committee has no power to alter the work-permit impasse and make an exception for our late applications. Lynne-Anne is furrow-browed with frustration and says we have to go and meet the minister in charge first thing tomorrow morning.

A production executive from IMG in Jo'burg arrives and thinks he might be able to help sway things favourably tomorrow.

When I question him as to why IMG were not able to pay the small charge to get the office phone connected for four weeks, he has no answer, which telegraphs precisely how effective he is going to be as an executive 'presence'.

The Theatre Club committee are angry about their rental contract not being completed yet. No sooner is one fire dampened down than another flares up somewhere too close by.

Michelle Maxwell calls from Jo'burg. Her soap-opera filming schedule has changed and she's no longer available, so I ask Kim Borrell, the best local amateur actress I knew back then, to play her part instead.

Octogenarians Johnny and Stella Masson, who were in the Colonial Service, kindly agree to let us borrow his OBE medal, pith helmet, ceremonial sword and some sixties biscuit tins for props.

## 2 June 2004

Five days to start of shooting. Two weeks after I was instructed to beg the DCMS for late-application leeway, I'm now about to beg the 'fat old Swazi guy', to quote our absent 'leader', for clemency over our work permits. At precisely 8.30 a.m., Lynne-Anne, an IMG production executive and I pitch up at the Ministry as instructed.

The Minister wastes no time whatsoever and detonates a half-hour bombardment directed solely at me. It's the single most humiliating and abusive bollocking I have *ever* suffered. It boils down to 'YOU WILL NOT START FILMING ON MONDAY THE 7th'. He is incandescent that there has been no follow-up or paperwork to the meeting with the French producer and South African production facilities co-ordinator since the recce in February. 'Why was there no contact? Why was there no one in Swaziland to keep things on track? Where were you, *Grant*? Why were you not here, *Grant*? Why was I not informed, *Grant*?' He is unstoppable and unplacatable.

My feeble attempt to explain that the finances have collapsed and been resurrected, that this is the producers' responsibility and not professional neglect on my part, goes for a Burton. His voice is now two decibels below full shout. '*His Majesty* is angry with you, *the Ministry* is angry with you, the head of *police* is angry with you! You will have to pay a very big fine! YOU CANNOT START WORK ON MONDAY.' I plead, explain, beg, grovel, but all to no avail. 'No, no, no, no, no, no, *no!*'

In the poisonous silence that follows, from somewhere far off, I hear these words come quietly and calmly out of my mouth: 'Minister, with the greatest respect, no offence was intended. I am profoundly sorry that this has happened. As we do not have work permits in advance of filming, we are unable to delay beyond the 7th. We will lose our main actors, who are booked to start other films in August. We will not be able to make the film in Swaziland, and I regret to say that the country will not earn any money whatsoever because the film will have to shut down. We are *completely* at fault and I understand your position entirely. Thank you for agreeing to meet us so early in the morning. I am very sorry that there is nothing I can do, sir.'

I know this is brinkmanship. I know there is no alternative. I know that the likely reality is that it's all over before it's even properly begun.

I look at Lynne-Anne, we stand and beg leave to depart.

At which the Minister stalls us, and after repeating that it's impossible to start filming *until* the permits are processed – which can take weeks – he changes tack and says that he will convene another meeting with his committee this afternoon to discuss the matter further, and that I should be on standby in case I am summoned by the King to explain the situation. He asks for my mobile number and the three of us squelch out of his office like broke-backed crabs.

'You tell me, Lynne-Anne – *tell* me I'm not imagining things, but that this has to be the worst full-frontal bollocking you've ever encountered?'

She concurs. I call Paris and for once manage to get straight through to the absentee MC, whose blood I am ready to *boil* at this point.

Her immediate response? 'So you *believe* this minister? You believe him and not me?'

'That's not the fucking *point*! It doesn't matter *who* I believe, the point is, he says we *cannot* start shooting on the 7th *because we do not have any work permits*. That is where we are at!'

'But the King gave us permission.'

'To film here yes, but we require *work permits*.'

I slug the phone to Lynne-Anne to explain, who is subjected to an earful about how unappreciative and ungrateful I've been for all her producing efforts and that she is ready to 'throw in the towel and pull the plug'.

I cannot credit this insanity, and I start laughing. You could not *invent* this stuff, it's *that* daft. 'You believe him and not me?' rattles around my cranium like a superannuated boiled sweet.

Whichever way you cut it, *we* are the ones needing a stay of execution and immediate grace and favour in the bending of work-permit rules and regulations.

The idea that you could cajole a government minister in London or Paris to make an exception to these procedures at such short notice is plainly ludicrous, and the disrespect of MC saying just go and speak to that 'fat old Swazi guy' speaks volumes about her assumption that as a minister in a small third-world country, he will bend to first-world pressure. I feel acutely embarrassed to be associated with this.

We head for the production office in a state of shock. What's next? The faces inside tell all. The make-up carnet in London, which has been ready to fly for five days, hasn't left Heathrow. The cash deposit to guarantee the hire of the steam train for the penultimate day of the shoot is now three days late. The cash for the lighting equipment trucks to leave Jo'burg has not materialized yet, and the drivers are refusing to move till they're paid.

But in the wake of what's just happened, all of this is mere tiddlywinks. I plonk down on the pavement in the warm wintry sun and wonder what's best to do while waiting on word from the committee.

I call Sindi Nxumalo, who is playing Regina, the Swazi housekeeper, and with whom I was at school, to ask if she can think of anything diplomatic to do. She kindly promises to try.

Spend the remainder of the day doing further camera recces in a half daze of will it, won't it. Charlie is having none of it and says, 'We *will* make this, no matter what.' Gary too believes that something will give at the very last minute.

The Minister calls at 4.45 p.m. and we are summoned back to his office to hear the results of the meeting, which are:

a) Work-permit applications must be lodged by this evening/first thing tomorrow morning and will take a minimum of a week to process.
b) Each location will require police personnel.
c) Cannot start shooting on Monday the 7th June as scheduled.
d) Letters requesting location permissions must be delivered immediately to the commissioner.

e) The licence to film in the country is 10,000 emalangeni (£1,000) and must be signed off and paid for tomorrow.

f) A meeting must be convened with the tax office to clarify payments.

He is at pains to point out that it is the film company who has caused this delay and not the Swazi government, who cannot be expected to bend laws because our applications are so late. We leave his office and Lynne-Anne calls MC to report the results. Stunned silence.

The French production manager, Martin, has recovered, but will only arrive in the country on Friday evening with the British and French cast and crew forms, medical certificates and confirmation that we are not importing any ex-criminals. This is too late for the Police, Immigration and Labour Committee, which meets only once a week. So by this reckoning, everything will be delayed by a minimum of two weeks.

The best I can hope for is to be granted an audience with the King, who was in Malaysia but has now returned, at which I will have to beg permission to start shooting *whilst* the applications are being processed, as long as they are paid for in advance. I put in the request.

The hours tick by. At 8.30 p.m. I call Gary to ask about any progress with the equipment trucks in Jo'burg. A total impasse.

At 9 p.m., Qhawe Mamba, head of the King's video news coverage, calls to say that I must be at the palace at 2 p.m. tomorrow.

Is this a reprieve? Whichever and whatever, my nerves are so shredded that I lie face down on my bed and blub like a bitter baby.

Phone home and Joan says the actors are in a panic as they all have to show up at a police station to get fingerprinted and pay for certificates to prove that they're not ex-cons.

Chris Curling calls at 10.20 p.m. from London, explaining that the reason MC is not here in Swaziland is because she has so many deals still to sign off on in Paris. I suspect she resents Chris's intervention as go-between co-producer, possibly as she feels her power is being usurped, and demands of him that I make an effort to welcome her when she finally arrives out here as she is the main producer.

Slept like an insomniac.

### 3 June 2004

Well at *least* the Minister has not vetoed our chances of filming outright. Or so we think until we receive the licence contract issued by the committee at 11 a.m. demanding a further fee of a million emalangeni (£100,000) on top of the E10,000 licence fee, to cover the costs of administration, filming rights, policing, use of 'scenery of Swaziland' etc. Plus a proviso that the film be vetted before it is commercially released.

This fee and the proviso have never been mentioned before, and as this is the first film ever made here, there is no precedent, so they have us over the proverbial barrel. This is surreal blackmail territory and not even remotely feasible.

The Minister calls at 11.30. 'Did you get the contract?'

'Yes, thank you, sir. Do you have any news from Immigration and the Commissioner of Police yet, sir?'

The Minister replies that his meeting with them has gone very well and that they are willing to allow us to start filming on Monday if we can guarantee that the South African crew's applications are in by today, and the British and French papers delivered by tomorrow evening.

I express heartfelt gratitude for this leniency and 'generous' reprieve. However, the million emalangeni demand hovers unmentioned, and I assume he thinks that we will pay it.

'Meet me at your hotel at 2 p.m. before you meet with His Majesty,' he says.

I wonder what it'd be like to be back home in London this weekend weeding the garden. Like Jacobean courtiers, we say to each other, 'Everything depends on the meeting with the King.'

While waiting at the hotel as instructed, we get a call to say that the Minister will not be meeting us first as he has been summoned to the palace ahead of us. It strikes me that if the Minister has His Majesty's endorsement of the million-emalangeni demand, we are well and truly stewed.

Finally, at 3.45, Mavis Litchfield, the King's uber-organizer, calls and says to get to Lozitha Palace immediately. We pile into the rental car and drive hell for leather towards our fate. On the radio Bob Marley is singing 'Everything's gonna be all right' and we hope out loud that the man is *right*.

The protocol is that everyone is kept waiting for anything between one hour and eight to meet with the King. The Minister and Qhawe Mamba are in the waiting room, having been there since *noon*. Mavis appears and we are all taken through for our audience. The King greets me with real warmth and no sign of anger whatsoever, insisting that I sit next to him on a matching throne, whilst the Minister and Qhawe traditionally sit shoeless on the floor.

He asks me to explain the reasons for the delay in making the film. Flying by the seat of my pants, I do so, after which the King says, 'So what is it you are asking me to do for you?'

'We are asking for your blessing to let filming go ahead, and that we can negotiate fees for the various government departments that we can reasonably pay, as we simply do not have one million emalangeni as stipulated by the Minister today.'

His wide-eyed reaction suggests that it's the first he has heard about this, and he immediately asks the Minister to explain how this fee breaks down.

The Minister, in clear discomfort, says that at least half a million will be required to pay for policemen to be drafted in from around the country to deal with the security of the film unit. I mention that we already have a security company contracted to the unit and will need between five to ten policemen at *most* to control traffic and onlookers for street and vegetable-market scenes which will both be filmed on the same day.

When further costs are quoted for copyright on 'scenery' and such, it is patently clear that this fee is not tenable. The Minister suggests that His Majesty must not be troubled with these details, but I reiterate that we simply cannot pay a million and will have to abandon everything. I feel like I am begging for my life here.

The King says that a realistic and reasonable figure must be renegotiated because he would like the film to go ahead. His approbation is unequivocal and I am overwhelmed by this reprieve; the power of an absolute monarch never seemed so sweet.

Outside in the anteroom I thank the dyspeptic Minister profusely, whilst Lynne-Anne arranges to meet his committee to renegotiate terms.

I get into the car laughing and levitating and everyone is on their mobiles to transmit the good news. *Even* MC has the momentary grace to say thank you to Lynne-Anne. I can't stop shaking, with the sheer stress and pressure of it all.

I meet Charlie, Gary, Alex and Alan to go through everything I missed in the production meeting they held while we were at the palace. Finally escape into the loo and break down, sobbing uncontrollably from the sheer relief of our royal reprieve.

### *4 June 2004*

Just when we thought we were *safe*, meltdown – the DCMS co-production requirements stipulate the *exact* number of crew members allowed from each co-producing country, and no prizes for guessing that someone has somehow managed to *overlook* this crucial fact and has gone ahead and employed South African key crew members instead. None of whom can now legally stay. You would assume that after the DCMS Damocles in Cannes, MC, as the main producer, would have had the sense to make absolutely sure that we do *not* contravene *any* of their requirements!

Without a producer present, it is left to Lynne-Anne to try and deal with this debacle, which is further complicated by the fact that her husband, Sven Vosloo, is the South African focus puller who has just driven 1,200 miles up from Cape Town and will have to be 'fired' before we even begin, simply because he is not an English or French citizen. This applies to key members of the camera and art departments, as well as members of the production-management team.

The day is taken up with phone calls back-and-forthing trying to find English or French passport holders who happen to live in neighbouring South Africa, happen to be film technicians and happen to be free to get to Swaziland at a day's notice to start shooting on Monday! No pressure, then!

Gabriel Byrne arrives and I do my best to make sure that he knows nothing about any of these upheavals. It's great to have him actually here at last. His request for a converter plug to get his laptop up and running is curiously appealing – this is something that can be done *without* bending, grovelling, lying or begging.

The majority of the technical crew have now arrived, including the newly recovered French production manager Martin Jaubert. Everyone's in the bar at 6 p.m. Alex Oakley gets a call from Chrissie Baker and Sheena Napier, who are at Heathrow due to board their flight, saying that in spite of giving Martin Jaubert and the French production office a week's notice about the excess-baggage costs for the first week's worth of make-up, wigs and costumes luggage, Martin just gave them £100 in cash and advised them to 'put the rest on your personal credit cards and get reimbursed later'. The excess baggage fee clocks in at £3,000. As neither Chrissie nor Sheena have been paid *anything* yet for their weeks of pre-production work, they are in no mood or position to fork this out.

For a moment it looks as if Alex might fist Jaubert's head into the nearest available wall, but he restrains himself and opts for an undiluted verbal tirade, to which Jaubert's response is, 'It's not my responsibility.'

Chris Curling is finally called and agrees to get Scion to pay for sending Andrew McEwan (the second assistant director, who has been running around London all week getting the cast's medical and police certificates) with the excess baggage on Saturday's flight tomorrow night, enabling Chrissie and Sheena to board their plane at the very last minute. They will thus arrive here *without* their gear and will have to wait till Sunday, then work on their one day off to get everything prepped and ready in time for Monday.

More phone calls and last-minute attempts to salvage the key crew members under threat, all to no avail. Convene an emergency meeting in my bedroom at 11 p.m. and have the gruesome task of telling people that they are to be replaced forthwith. The meeting lasts two hours and grown men and women are in tears. Everyone is exhausted, feels abused, insulted and disbelieving that they have turned down other work and travelled the distance to work on this film. Martin Jaubert, the sole representative of the French producer, does not utter a *single* word throughout.

Lynne-Anne is in such a state that she threatens to resign, having held everything together here for the past four fraught pre-production weeks, and I beg her to sleep on it and decide by midday tomorrow.

I collapse into bed, exhausted by this week of hell. The prospect of seven weeks of shooting seems like a doddle compared to all these upheavals. Instead of starting the film in a state of prepared calm, my nerves are nuked.

REG and Gabriel Byrne.

'Stay sweet as you are': Miranda Richardson, Gabriel Byrne and Nicholas Hoult.

Miranda Richardson and Gabriel Byrne.

Nicholas Hoult and Emily Watson.

Emily Watson and Gabriel Byrne.

Karen Jones:
script supervisor supreme.

REG, Gary Williamson
and Charlie Watson.

Jack Waters, Emily,
REG, Ronelle Schmidt,
Gabriel, Nicholas.

Julie Walters.

Charlie Watson in charge of the low-loader.

Gabriel Byrne and Miranda Richardson in 'ice-cream suits'.

'Independence' – a.k.a. how to make sixty people look like six thousand.

Swazi 'Independence' maidens.

Gabriel Byrne and Miranda Richardson.

Sc 29 D5 cont into
Julie CO·ee

Gabriel Byrne.

SC
56
N12

Reduring
round
eyes
wave
cheeks

Nicholas Hoult.

Zac Fox.

Emily Watson.

REG, Karen Jones and
Miranda Richardson.

Gabriel Byrne.

Gabriel Byrne.

Nicholas Hoult, REG
and Gabriel Byrne.

Ralph View                  Dude
                                   down

Ralph + Vernon

Vernon                Ralph
           Chales ♥ June.

Hold on full face for 16 seconds then
45 second Track in on Ralph. track.

S-120         Car

Jessica   Vernon Monica Robyn Ralph Maisie
Wills.

♪ " Cuddle, Puddle, Cuddle Puddle "
Cuddle, Puddle, Cuddle, Puddle

SC121 Cuddle Puddle.

all jump in. Ralph

Mowat + Ralph.

Wide angle revelry.

Gwen's Ship.

Gwen
♪ 'We're all Buggered!'

'We're all Buggered'
CHORUS.

"The Big Splash."

Nicholas Hoult and Gabriel Byrne.

Sid Mitchell and Nicholas Hoult.

*Camelot*: Julie Walters and REG.

*Camelot*: backstage.

The world premiere – Gabriel Byrne and Emily Watson (eight months pregnant with Juliet).

The cast at the Edinburgh Film Festival – Nicholas Hoult, Gabriel Byrne, REG, Zac Fox, Julian Wadham, Sid Mitchell and Olivia Grant.

## *5 June 2004*

7 a.m. departure for Mbabane with Pierre Aïm to view the camera tests done in London weeks ago. Get to the Royal Swazi Convention Centre at 8.30 to find that there is no projectionist and the door is locked. Further crossed wires. As it is the only film projector in the country, we have no choice but to scramble around the staff quarters of the hotel trying to locate the missing man. At 9.30 we find him at a local garage where he works, and get him back to the convention centre. Finally, the tests spool forth and within a minute I am ready to stop and return to Pigg's Peak. Pierre's idea to do one version in 'normal colour' and another in 'bleached-out' yellows is clear – the sepia yellow bleached look is *everything* I don't want the film to look like. I make an instant decision to reject this.

Pelt back north to Pigg's Peak to meet Gabriel Byrne for rehearsals. He is very jet-lagged, and has no idea that crew have had to be replaced. Lynne-Anne has negotiated with the 'departees' to work for the first four days until their new French replacements arrive and, mercifully, she agrees to stay on for the whole shoot. But the decision is extremely painful for her as her husband is now 'out' and she is emotionally charged.

The cost of paying everyone off, plus the excess-baggage costs and flying out Andrew McEwan, will doubtless incur further shooting restrictions and cuts in the weeks ahead. *All* of which could and should have been avoided.

The calm oasis of sitting with Gabriel discussing the subtext of his role, the history behind each character and incident, listening and noting down his myriad ideas and opinions about his character and the script, is somewhere that I had doubted we would ever get to. His attention to every nuance and detail, and his reading of the story as being essentially about loss and unrequited love, reminds me *why* we are all here.

3 p.m. Miranda Richardson, Nicholas Hoult, Sid Mitchell, who plays Vernon, the best friend of Ralph, and Zac Fox arrive, along with Chrissie Baker, her assistant Cheryl Mitchell, Sheena Napier and her assistant Tamar Zaig. All of them are thrilled to be in Africa for the first time.

Play tennis with Charlie at 6 p.m. Am incredibly grateful for his unwavering support and steadfast determination to ensure that everything will run tickety-boo.

Alex and Lynne-Anne produce the first call sheet. We are *actually* going to start shooting at dawn on Monday – despite the absence of the producer, and despite the fact that the finance is still not officially signed off. The managers of the Orion Pigg's Peak Hotel have organized a poolside barbecue for the cast and crew, which is a much-appreciated and welcome getting-to-know-you introduction for everyone – English, Swazi, South African and French.

### 6 June 2004

6 a.m. run in the beautiful mountains – cold, steely blue and clear. 7 a.m. dash to the northern border post along with Charlie, Gary and Pierre to get our two-week visitor-entry visas re-stamped. The farce of filling in the forms and crossing into South Africa, turning around and doing it all in reverse momentarily loses its funny side when the guy operating the gate starts asking questions, which we bluff our way through, then zoom off on the road to Maguga Dam to recce locations for the numerous car scenes.

Rush back to Pigg's Peak to meet Gabriel and Miranda for rehearsals at 11 a.m. We discuss every aspect of the script for three hours, without ever reading any of the lines. They worked together in David Cronenberg's *Spider*, which is a distinct advantage as there is an automatic shorthand, or so it seems to me. Miranda is supremely unsentimental in her approach to her role, which instantly establishes the dynamic of their fictional relationship. Having cast them without the reassurance of the three of us meeting together at least once before today, it is an enormous relief to witness their obvious chemistry together. During our discussion, I am aware of the script being absorbed and transferred to the actors, a weird handover process whereby something that is so acutely personal to me is taken over by these two talented people.

2 p.m. and up to the Boshimela house location for a walk-through of where each and every scene will be filmed, props inspection and choices made about which cigarette lighter, glass and chair is to be used. Into the make-up trailer where Chrissie, Ashley and Cheryl are wigging, back-combing, cutting and testing their war paint on each actor, their baggage having arrived just in the nick of.

Electricians and riggers set up lighting in the rafters of the thatched roof, cables snake along every corridor, through doors and windows out into the garden to the generator van, a vast marquee is set up in the field beside the catering trailer, the wardrobe truck is crammed with costumes, and a Wild West circle of battered old caravans is formed for the actors to get changed in and rest. It's a circus. Everyone is scrambling and readying for tomorrow, and the excitement and frenzy of it all is an adrenalin rush.

I am so excited I can hardly breathe – it's taken *five* years to get to this point, and it genuinely feels like this is everything I was destined in my dreams to be doing. I *should* be panicked and freaked, but I suspect that the rodeo ride of the past months has been so chaotic and painful, that the surety of actually shooting the script is what's stopping me from going AWOL. Charlie suggested that the absence of the incompetent MC in the first week of shooting might well prove to be a godsend. No question!

Dinner in the hotel and the English crew have taken over the bar.

The French eat together in the dining room. Two-hour phone call home, and my wife and daughter's love and support through all of these upheavals is nothing less than monumental. Chris Curling calls from London to say that I need to sign a faxed copy of the new amendment to my writer's contract which assigns copyright to both Scion *and* Loma Nasha. Whilst wishing me the best of luck, he warns that the DCMS application has not been officially accepted yet and 'hopes' we can start shooting tomorrow.

'*Nothing* is going to stop me now, Chris. Short of Sherman tanks invading, we *will* start shooting tomorrow.'

# SHOOTING

## 7 June 2004

*'Anything and everything is possible if you dream.'* – Richard E. Grant

Alex Oakley inserts this quote at the top of the first day's call sheet.

First day of shooting. Slept seven hours! Can't remember when I last did that. 5.30 a.m. wake up and run. Nerves. Shakes. 6.30 breakfast in the marquee. The whole army of a hundred are here. Everyone gets a name-tag. I asked Richard Curtis for some director advice before I flew out. He was unequivocal: get good caterers, and ensure the camera turns over *before* 11 a.m. The food is wonderful and despite inevitable technical delays, it being the first day, we turn over by 9.15 a.m.! With the winter daylight hours there is no time to faff about.

Very strange not to spend the first two hours of the day in the make-up and wardrobe trailers with other actors. Seeing Gabriel in the full white ice-cream colonial uniform looking so like my father proves emotional for me. Miranda is similarly decked out in a cream fitted suit and perfectly coiffed blonde wig. Zac Fox is dressed and combed to doppelgänger perfection, wearing blue contact lenses without any fuss whatsoever, extraordinarily relaxed and self-possessed for someone making his first film – a mixture of being a very young-looking thirteen-year-old with the focus of a veteran. He's excited but also very concentrated, technically adept at hitting his floor marks and precisely repeating his actions, which will make Karen's continuity job a relative doddle.

Karen is the ideal script supervisor/continuity accomplice, sitting beside me at the camera monitor, always encouraging and acutely aware of everything that is going on. She is blessed with innate compassion and diplomacy and knows instinctively how to speak to actors about their continuity and dialogue deviations.

I wonder whether anyone will laugh, or yelp 'Pull the other one' when my moment to call 'action' arrives. Not a peep, and we are off and running. Charlie has assumed military control of proceedings.

Knowing as they do that they will be replaced by French nationals at the end of the week, the professionalism and generosity of the key South African crew members is something that I will always feel indebted to them for. They seem as excited and committed as everyone else on our first day of filming.

The circular trajectory for me – my first experiences of 'theatre' were with a painted shoebox and stick-figures when I was seven, then a full-scale marionette theatre in my teens, to a proscenium-arched theatre, television, then movies and now watching actors playing out my fictionalized adolescent life on a shoebox-sized monitor – is nothing short of miraculous to me at this moment.

Charlie has advised me to get the first satisfactory print of the opening camera set-up as soon as possible to establish that there will be no farting about. This is a conundrum: on the one hand the actors need to feel as relaxed as possible and free to give of their best, but on the other there is constant pressure to move on in order to stay on schedule.

The hours of sitting around with Gabriel and Miranda discussing the script, subtext and background history pay off in the concentrated and utterly focused commitment each brings to their roles. Miranda delivers at full force on take one, setting the benchmark for their confrontational relationship. We are contractually obliged to shoot all of her scenes in the first and fifth weeks; the bonus is that we are starting in chronological order. It requires a few takes for Gabriel to match her intensity, but there is no doubting how instantly believable they are. The relief is enormous and the no-nonsense concentration of their playing creates real excitement amongst the crew.

# SHOOTING

Two scenes completed by lunchtime, and the atmosphere is as convivial as you could hope for. All the upheavals and sense of going into the 'unknown' these past months are instantly replaced by the familiarity of the filming process, and any nerves felt up front have been eased.

Lynne-Anne spends the whole afternoon negotiating with the government committee, and despite the midway wobble of being asked to pay half a million emalangeni (£50,000) for police *petrol* costs, I kid you not, the final fee is settled at E180,000 (£18,000).

Chris Curling calls to confirm that the DCMS application *has* been granted, meaning that the film will now be fully financed. First day's filming completed! In bed by 10 p.m.!

## *8 June 2004*

Overcast, windy and cold. With very little leeway for bad weather in the schedule it is sheer luck that we are shooting dining-room scenes all day.

I'd had dinner with legendary director Mike Nichols earlier in the year and asked his advice: 'Actors can always act faster than they think they can.' In the spirit of which, we shoot quickly, and only the number of takes required to nail the scene. Occasionally there is a 'bonus' take for them to try whatever they want to, and sometimes 'one for Mike'. The energy generated by speaking the dialogue a gnat's faster often prompts something which will hopefully prove valuable when it comes to editing.

The first scene is the final confrontation between mother and father, where Lauren/Miranda speaks directly to her husband Harry/Gabriel for the first time in nine months. Miranda is different in every take and varies between a skittish laughing cruelty and barely suppressed venom, all delivered with the absolute minimum of direction. She requires a word or two at most between takes, and does not play for an ounce of sympathy. Bracing and brutal.

It's weird to be recreating a condensed fictionalized scene from my childhood and to see Gabriel Byrne instinctively 'mirroring' my father's reactions.

As the dining room is very narrow and claustrophobic, crammed with equipment, cables and lights, I've asked the crew to be as quiet as possible between camera and lighting set-ups so that the actors' concentration is not disrupted. The team spirit and respect shown by the crew is heartening.

After lunch, we shoot the telephone conversation in which the father begs the mother to come back. Watching Gabriel and Zac playing my father and me hurtles me back to 1967. Pain has no sense of time. It feels as raw now as it did back then.

Every time Pierre Aïm tries to set up a shot that is 'good for the light' or 'good for the set', I have to stick to the dictum that guided me throughout the writing of the script – *everything* has to be from the boy's point of view. It proves to be a foolproof compass and precludes anything unnecessary or arty-farty.

Ian Roberts, whom I have known since university days in Cape Town in the seventies, arrives to play the small but crucial role of adulterer. I arrange to meet with him and Miranda in the bar in the evening so that they can get to know each other as quickly as possible, seeing as they have to bonk each other all day tomorrow, albeit fully clothed on the front seat of a car. Luckily they talk non-stop.

I'm aware of Gabriel sitting across from them, talking to Sindi Nxumalo but subtly clocking his fictional 'competition'.

# SHOOTING

## 9 June 2004

Gary and his team have created a mini-studio in an empty barn, replete with cloth blackouts and the car seats of the 1967 Mercedes mounted on tyre platforms with levers underneath to simulate the car moving. This is for the opening scene in which eleven-year-old Ralph 'wakes up' and discovers his mother shagging his father's best friend on the front seat.

The deconstruction of it all makes for a jokey atmosphere and any worries about Zac being potentially embarrassed by the bonking is immediately dispelled by his total lack of any inhibition. And the fact he is filmed in isolation without actually seeing anything!

Miranda and Ian arrive late afternoon as we can only shoot this scene once it's dark, as the exterior needs to be lit by the car's headlights. Miranda reports that she dreamt about Gabriel wearing a dress and make-up, which has us all marvelling and teasing her for being a true method actress.

How do you direct two of your friends to shag each other? Simple: 'You guys know what to do, don't you?' Without flinching, they maul each other with the conviction of lifelong adulterers. Comic relief is supplied by instructions to 'Get your bum higher, Miranda,' and 'Groan more, please, Ian.'

Tension builds up between Pierre Aïm, Karen Jones and me regarding the all-important 'invisible' line-crossing rules which dictate where the camera should be placed in order to match actors' eye-lines in the editing. We have come to the conclusion that as Pierre usually works as director of photography in charge of the lighting and framing of each shot, he is less used to operating the actual camera, which may be a source of confusion. They are usually two separate jobs, but he is doing both.

Karen and I have decided that I need to do very basic storyboards, mapping out the shot list for the day in cartoons so that there is no time wasted arguing or leaving room for misunderstanding or language shortcomings. These are to be gone through with Pierre at breakfast so that we are all working from the same page.

Nick Hoult's first day, and it's hard to believe he is only six months older than Zac, but he's six foot three already and only fourteen. He's very nervous. I suggest he channel all this anxiety into his first scene, in which he has just run away from his mother and pelted six miles to get home to tell his father the *real* reason for his mum's return. Nick runs around the garden a few times, which goes some way to easing him in. From the first time I met and screen-tested him, Nick required the least amount of directorial input and he delivers every time without any fuss. Whether by instinct, talent or whatever else it is which makes someone 'believable', he is always truthful and 'in the moment'. The less discussion the better. A marvel.

Miranda's intelligence and instincts are formidable and she can intimidate people with her sometimes prickly responses, so it is very welcome when she announces in the bar that we are 'a heavenly bunch of people and I'll really miss not being here for the next four weeks'.

Went to bed early to do the storyboards. The past months of ceaseless tensions and worry are catching up.

### 11 June 2004

Perfect weather. The air at Boshimela is champagne-sparkly clean. The house is set in a saddle position on the mountains, with this incredible sweeping view stretching endlessly into the hazy distance. Its serenity and timelessness have affected everyone.

Seeing my crude storyboards becoming three-dimensional reality while shooting the scenes of Lauren/Miranda's return in the middle of the night is very satisfying.

Gabriel constantly questions, challenges and explores every scene and line of dialogue he has, rooting out the ambiguity and resistance, offering up ideas and suggestions as if living his part all the time. *Nothing* escapes his attention. Ralph/Nicholas is scripted to put on Nat King Cole and get his estranged parents dancing together. Gabriel suggests that the set-up be done in total silence, making it more awkward and mysterious, so that when the music comes on, it can weave its spell in 'real' time. This may sound like a trivial detail, but Gabriel's re-working of it is transforming.

However, as acutely tuned as he is to the emotional depths of his role, he is endearingly near-dyspraxic when it comes to handling props, dancing or remembering where he put his cup down. He is aware of this foible and is so disarmingly funny and self-deprecating about it that he doesn't take umbrage when we assign the props department to be on permanent 'Gabe alert'. He is also genetically armed with an arsenal of Dublin charm which draws women of all ages to him at all times, wherever he is.

The combination of a fourteen-year-old boy playing Nat King Cole's 'Stay As Sweet As You Are' and silently manoeuvring his estranged parents to dance together again gets 'continuity' Karen crying. Gabriel confirms that this is the dream of every child of divorced parents – reconciliation. Rapprochement. Having had psychoanalysis for eighteen months some years back, I know that this desire to rewrite and reconnect the impossible never goes away. How perfect that I am able to do so in a film version.

There is a police *presence* at lunch and their collective appetite is enormous. A government-committee member asks after my father, and I assume she knew him way back when, but it transpires she means Denholm Elliott, whose hapless son I played in *Killing Dad*, which has recently been on Swazi TV. No amount of explanation or denial can convince her that the late, great Denholm is no relation.

We bid a sad farewell to the South African camera crew, who so valiantly got us up and running without rancour, now replaced by their newly arrived French counterparts, Delphine, Tao, Etienne and Denys. Pierre Aïm is very pleased as he is now able to communicate at speed in his own language. The changeover is seamless.

Less seamless is the fact that having been assured that we would get rushes every couple of days, there is no sign of any. The 'logic' of sending the footage to Paris to be processed and then flown back to Swaziland, when there are laboratories in Jo'burg, a mere five-hour drive away, which would enable us to see them the next day, is something that the French are unable to justify satisfactorily. Not only is it inefficient, it's very costly and, more frustratingly, has resulted in us nearly completing the first week of shooting with no 'evidence' to watch and readjust to.

### 12 June 2004

Freezing 4.45 a.m. departure to Maguga Dam for all the interior car and drive-by scenes. Charlie is in his element – first major location move, vehicles, action, *Boy's Own* stuff involving an army of crew, technical vehicles and a low-loader truck on which the car and actors are secured to simulate driving, followed by another truck with the camera and video playback monitor.

Sid Mitchell's first day of filming and though twenty-four, he looks fifteen.

'How come you're so tanned, Sid?'

'I'm a window cleaner,' is his totally unexpected reply. 'That's what I do when I'm between jobs.' His charm and lack of any la-di-dah wins over everyone he meets within a nanosecond.

The technical fandango involved in strapping the car onto the trailer, getting it lit, microphoned and walkie-talkied up, having the police set up the roadblock and the actors rehearsed, takes an age. However, trussed up in blankets, Karen and I are treated to an impromptu 'radio' show by Zac and Gabriel through our headphones. Sitting in the car waiting to shoot, they start off by comparing farting stories, followed by Zac mercilessly grilling Gabriel about who he thinks are really great actors.

Zac's ability when he hears 'Action!' to switch from the middle of a detailed fartological epic to the scripted dialogue about his character's mother's recent departure is astonishing in someone so young.

I keep having to remind Gabriel to turn the steering wheel to make it *look* as if he is driving, with the result that he goes from not moving the steering wheel at all to giving it the full St Vitus's dance treatment, which makes us all fall about.

At 9.30 a.m. at the end of the first week of shooting, MC finally pitches up on set and says – 'Give me a *hug*!'

'What for?'

I am incredulous that having suffered the *nightmare* of the past months of pre-production and her appalling lack of communication, she could dare *kid* herself that I might suddenly puppy forth and oblige her! Only the small French fraternity give her the welcome she clearly expects.

Most producers would have had the grace to introduce themselves to the crew and thank everyone for the work they have put in, but not this one. She seems to assume that because she is credited as producer on the call sheet, this automatically confers status and respect. I look forward to watching how long it takes for everyone to rumble that bollocks.

Mercifully she doesn't stay beyond lunch. Every last minute of fast-receding daylight is maximized and Charlie is hoarse from shouting out instructions above the engine noise. Cars are loaded on and taken off the trailer, re-rigged and filmed all day long, with the actors having to repeat very short scenes of dialogue endlessly, with different sections of the road as scenic background. Their patience and forbearance is invaluable, as there are only so many times you can say something without it starting to come out as gobbledegook.

Wrap at 5.30 as the sun dips quickly behind the mountains, and everyone cheers at having completed the first week on schedule.

Played five games of tennis at 6.30, then had to give up. Knees went wobbly like an old boxer. I'm shattered, but have a huge sense of achievement at having cracked the first week, the crew changes and the first major location move.

Quiet dinner with newly arrived Emily Watson and her writer husband, Jack Waters. Her calm, contained and introspective manner suddenly unleashes itself when she trills, 'We're in *Swaziland!*' with such unbridled excitement that all pocket-book psychology goes out of the window.

End-of-first-week party in the Wasabi restaurant. First time every nationality on the crew has *really* integrated socially, everyone dancing with the abandoned conviction that a day off guarantees. Bed at 1 a.m. Phone home to discover that my daughter is very ill. Feel abjectly awful at being so far away and unable to help.

### *13 June 2004*

*Swazi Sunday Times* headline: 'Government demands one million to block road for *Wah-Wah* filming', with a broadside about the government's 'preposterous' demand. All I can think is that someone's nose will be very out of joint this morning, which might threaten our progress. No phone call from anyone, though.

Join up with the cast and crew and hike through the surrounding forest to Phophonyane Falls for lunch. A case of hangovers and each to his own language today. First truly relaxed day we have all had together and the joking and joshing is non-stop. Without exception, *everyone* loves Swaziland so far and even though I've been away for half my life, it is a real kick to experience everyone's heartfelt enthusiasm.

SHOOTING

England versus France on the mega-TV screen in the bar fires up patriotic fervour, most especially in Sid Mitchell, Alex Oakley and Nick Hoult, all of whom arrive face-painted with the St George Cross.

And just when you least need 'em, here come two more executive producers from Jo'burg. Now that we are up and running, they're here to 'participate'. None of the cast or crew are fooled and they don't heed them much notice.

Went down the road to a restaurant full of Pigg's Peak foresters, who give us a Heath Robinson solution to the problem of trying to heat up the swimming pool for a forthcoming scene in which Nick and Sid have to swim as though it's midsummer. The head forester comes up with a master plan: set up an empty oil drum on bricks, build a fire underneath it, attach hoses at each end and circulate the water from the pool through the heated drum all night via a pump. He offers to supply the pump, hoses, wood and someone willing to keep the fire burning through the night – a much cheaper alternative to hiring a pool heater from across the border. It's a real reminder of small-scale life where someone is willing to muck in and help without expecting anything in return other than the sheer craic of it. Get back to the hotel and Gary is willing to try it, but looks understandably sceptical.

Phone home. Daughter has been put on penicillin.

*14 June 2004*

Established routine: run for forty minutes at dawn, eat a huge breakfast, lunch, no dinner, play tennis for an hour after wrap, half an hour in the bar with the cast and crew, then to my room to email, storyboard and plot the next day. Attempt seven hours' kip.

Shoot indoor night scenes all day long, with the windows blacked out by tarpaulins. The claustrophobia increases the ongoing tensions caused by the 'crossing the eye-line' debate between Karen and Pierre. The arguments are wasting time and causing confusion.

Gary has got his team welding, and testing the pump-and-drum contraption down at the pool, with intermittent spurting leaks, but all hands are on deck to make it work.

Inside, we set up a scene where Zac discovers Gabriel passed out in the drawing room listening to Al Bowlly singing 'Goodnight, Sweetheart' after his wife has left him. I have very strange déjà vu recreating this scene so precisely. It's one thing to write it, another entirely to see it realized. This was the night when, having seen my mother leave at dawn, I discovered my father so drunk he couldn't talk or walk, and I was forced to parent my pater as it were, covering him up with a blanket and trying to comfort him at the age of ten. I continued to 'cover up' and hide his alcoholism for the next thirty-three years.

Meet up with Emily during a technical break. She's here to have her hair coloured, and to familiarize herself with the house location, all the while speaking and asking questions in her adopted American accent. She does this without any fuss or fanfare, just meticulously working her way 'in' by what seems like osmosis.

Executive producer Joel Phiri calls at the end of the shooting day and requests a meeting with MC and me in the hotel lounge at 7 p.m.

'What's the agenda?'

'Just need to go through some stuff.'

We wait half an hour for her to show up, despite Joel's two phone calls to find out where she is. When she finally pitches up, sans apology, it transpires that she has called the meeting simply to haul me over the coals for sending a round-robin email to all the producers in which I singled out Chris Curling for especial thanks in the final week of pre-production for all his incredible support and availability.

'How *dare* you?' is her piping plea. 'Don't you know what I have been *doing*?'

'How could I? You never communicate anything.'

MC has the cheek to try and blame *me* for being non-communicado. Against everything I had pledged *not* to do, I unleash a forty-minute unvarnished undiluted catalogue of the daily nightmare we have all suffered over the past few weeks. A huge fucking relief really to finally tell her face to face *exactly* what has gone down.

'But you have to hear my story,' she yodels.

'Write it down, I've got too much work to do.'

This is war. Out and out. The promised rushes have *still* not shown up. Every time I query Martin Jaubert, all he can do is shrug and puff out some air.

### 15 June 2004

Slept four hours. Stressed and strained. Good news, though – the Heath Robinson machine has worked its magic and the pool temperature has gone up from twelve to twenty-four degrees overnight! I order some booze for the Trojan art department stalwarts who have pulled this off.

Joel Phiri has returned to Jo'burg and MC is now keeping a very wide berth. First take by 8.10 a.m. and completed seven camera/ lighting set-ups by lunch. *This* is the efficient pace at which we should keep working. Geoff (the camera stand-in) and I dive into the pool first to show willing. Bracing, but at least Nick and Sid know that *we* know what it's like. Filming outdoors has galvanized everybody and the mood is very up. Feel like I'm five again!

Checked my bank account. No payment. How to endear yourself to a cast and crew in ten easy lessons! If *I've* not been paid, I suspect no one else has either. Best not to ask and risk cast and crew upset.

Email Chris Curling to see if he can intervene and get the rushes processed in Jo'burg so we can have them back the following day.

### 16 June 2004

Emily Watson's first day, and both of us were nervous. Even though I worked with her on *Gosford Park* and we rehearsed and talked everything through in London, I was suddenly overwhelmed with inadequacy – how can I direct a double Oscar-nominated actor of her talent and stature? Lost my nerve for a couple of hours, intimidated and convinced I was making a complete arse of myself, but got more bullish and confident as the day progressed.

At least this is the first time Emily's character, Ruby, appears in the film, so she is starting with a clean slate, so to speak. Being English and playing the only American is daunting and requires a few takes for her confidence to get up to speed (and mine) but *every* time, Emily's Truthometer shines through. Her immediate rapport with Gabriel, both on and off screen, is something you dream will be 'there' on the day – and it *is*, by the bucket-load. They have never met before and only known each other for two days, yet here they are playing their first scene together and none of us are in any doubt that they are 'madly in love'.

Gary has only just got legal clearance to use the poster of Raquel Welch in *One Million Years B.C.* on Nick's bedroom wall. Despite requesting that MC get clearances secured well in advance of shooting, they had not been, with the result that it is finally cleared exactly *fifty* minutes before we are due to shoot. And she wonders why I lose all patience?!

The interior bedroom scene involves Emily giving Nick a welcome-home present of a pair of Pelham puppets. Gabriel cracks everyone up by forgetting to walk out of the scene as written, suddenly remembering halfway through, then lurching away. However, as he is supposed to be half sloshed, it's perfect. Elicits a round of applause.

Last scene to shoot is the end of a violently drunken tirade which is scheduled for the following week, but as we are already set up in the bedroom, we do it today out of sequence. It's a night scene in which Nick and Emily have barricaded themselves in Nick's bedroom whilst Gabriel violently bashes at the door, yelling blue murder.

Recreating the Jekyll and Hyde nature of my father's alcoholism – charmer by day, near unrecognizable monster after 9.30 p.m. – is grim. Instruct Oli and Graham, our props guys, to make the door banging as violent and noisy as they dare. Emily and Nick lean hard against it to prevent it opening and their heads ricochet with each blow. No direction required. Two long takes and their reactions are a pure and potent reminder of what it's like to be held prisoner in your own home by an addict out of control. Emily is clearly shaken up; we hug each other and don't have to say anything.

The ritual of running down the corridor and barricading my bedroom door, something which characterized my teenage years, is encapsulated in two takes and 'done' with. All the years of secrecy and attendant shame are levelled by being able to be honest and open about it all. Both actors give everything of themselves and once it's over, the crew are quick to compliment them.

My great friend and mentor Peter Capaldi emails me a warning about the rushes:

If you don't get it on the day, you don't get it in the rushes. I used to hope that some alchemy would transform things, and indeed the seductive charm of film makes everything look great. But if I hadn't made it happen on the day, the rushes weren't going to save my behookie [Scottish for 'arse'].

After a delay of nine days, which seems an eternity, the rushes are finally here. Usually only the director, producers and key crew see them, but in the spirit of Altman, everyone is invited to troop into the basement room to watch them on a TV. Except Gabriel, who waits in the bar as he hates to watch himself. It actually *looks* like a movie! When a take 'works' everyone recognizes it simultaneously. It's like an electric current going round the room. Despite the 'line-crossing' issues, Pierre's cinematography is stunning and I could not be more pleased.

Bruce Robinson always demanded that Paul McGann and I 'stamp ourselves onto the celluloid'. No half measures allowed. The sixth take of Gabriel's confrontation with Miranda on the veranda on the first day of shooting does precisely that. For me, it claims itself as the take to use when we come to edit. I wonder if editor Isabelle Dedieu will feel the same way.

Greece versus Spain followed by Russia versus Portugal on the big screen keeps the bar fully peopled. I am reluctantly waylaid and forced to deal with MC – surprise surprise, she cannot find *any* of the faxes from Warner Brothers' licensing department regarding the clip and poster usage of *A Clockwork Orange* that I provided her with four months ago. Being an anally retentive hoarder and seasoned anticipator of things not being followed through by her, I have brought all the copies with me and duly hand them over. I sometimes wonder what her fleet of assistants do?!

*17 June 2004*

Noon start. Very big day technically with a montage of building the puppet theatre, filmed with two cameras and no sound to a playback of a thirties song titled 'OK Toots' by Harry Roy and his Orchestra, shot in the garden to simulate a sixties Super 8 home movie. In the final shot where all the characters bob up their heads to appear in the puppet proscenium arch, Gabriel hilariously manages to pop up at the wrong time, *every* time.

After the supper break, it takes hours to set up camera tracks and to light the garden and pool for the confrontation between the revolver-waving father and son. Almost everyone who read the script asked if this scene really happened. Which it did, prompting questions as to how I could forgive my father after he tried to blow my brains out.

The answer is that having lived with his alcoholism for so long, I had become used to these extremes of character transformation and always knew this was not my *real* dad, but a monster who bore little resemblance to the sober father I loved and admired. I had also provoked him by emptying an entire case of his whisky down the drain in response to him being drunk and verbally abusive yet again, so his putting a gun to my head, extreme though it was, seemed part and parcel of the madness that overtakes *any* family suffering the insanity of addiction. I hid in the garden, but ran as soon as he flicked the garden lights on, leaving me no place to hide. He lurched up and, like a scene from a suburban Western, pointed the revolver at my head and said he was going to shoot me. The hysteria of the evening was such that when he actually threatened me face to face, I had had enough and quietly taunted him to 'get it all over with', goading him to have the courage of his drunken convictions. He finally fired a shot which missed, then pointed the gun at himself, and collapsed in self-pitying tears.

This scene is one that Pierre Aïm and I have prepared more than any other during the two location recces, yet now Pierre seems to have forgotten everything and the simplest close-up takes two hours to light. I think his trying to direct the lighting *and* operate the camera has undone him completely tonight. I agree with whatever he settles for and don't even try to push for what we had agreed on before. Charlie is shaking his head and muttering darkly about Waterloo and mutiny.

Emily insists on running barefoot from the house to the pool and stubs her toe so badly she is unable to do a second take. The front of her big toe is gashed and bleeding profusely. No sooner is she in the heated tent getting first aid than Gabriel, after only two takes of this crucial scene, falls and puts his back out. Feels like *MASH* in Swaziland. Whilst being attended to by the onset medic, Gabriel voices concern that Nick Hoult is not matching him in the dramatic shoot-out stakes, and I say that in reality, everything leading up to this moment had been so emotionally explosive, that I've purposely directed Nick to react in a low whisper, as I had done. Gabriel is not entirely convinced, so we do some alternative close-ups on Nick where he is more hysterical, but I know I won't use them.

This is the first time I felt I haven't achieved what is properly required for a scene, and it's infuriating. By midnight, I was too tired even to attempt to fight my corner and every time Pierre asked if I was happy, I concurred, convincing nobody.

Teeth-grindingly annoyed with myself.

Alex Oakley has taken to inserting jokes in the call sheet that cheer me up:

*Scene 121B. NIGHT SKY.*
Alien spacecraft lands on veranda. Gabriel Byrne offers them a drink. Nick Hoult is abducted.

### 18 June 2004

Mid-morning start due to the late finish last night. Puppet scenes in a work shed which Gary has transformed into a theatre, with an assortment of my original Pelham puppet collection augmented by borrowed and hired extras.

My original full-sized theatre was built in our garage and a perfect refuge when the drinking bouts got out of control. I held regular shows during the school holidays and was relentlessly mocked for 'playing with dolls' until someone discovered how much money I earned from each show. Then I had offers to 'help'. With no television in the country and very little organized entertainment for kids, I was guaranteed sell-out shows and crammed in sixty tots in rows along the floor. I sold homemade drinks in the interval, all of which paid for an extensive record and book collection over six years. This income was augmented by birthday-party shows using a portable scaled-down theatre. I never dreamt that thirty years later I would be back in Swaz with a hundred crew and cast to recreate this scenario and that I would operate one of the puppets being filmed.

It was a duck-to-water moment pulling the strings again. Sid and Nick are very adept and went for it with gusto. As the camera was set up to feature the puppets in close-up, I asked Pierre to shoot some extra footage of the painted backdrop and a line-up of all the puppets in order to cross-fade between them and the *Camelot* scenery and actual cast line-up later. We also filmed a huge close-up of Nick's mouth next to the mouth of the McBoozle puppet opening and closing to a recording of Gabriel yelling, 'Shudup, shudup, shudup, shuduuuuup.'

We moved to the front garden for the scene in which Nick is challenged by Emily to do his habitual facial tic, in an attempt to rid him of it. In reality, this involuntary facial contortion afflicted me the moment my mother left. I knew I was doing it, but couldn't stop. It manifested itself at precisely the moments it shouldn't have – standing in front of the class reading something out loud, or when taunted with the question 'Where's your mum?'

Good acting never ceases to amaze – Nick is fourteen years old and from a very stable, loving family background, but with the minimum of direction he expresses all this inarticulate pain in a brief but intense face-contorting competition with Emily. Her toe is bandaged today, whilst Gabriel is in a back brace.

Email from my agent before bed: 'Can you return to London for three days to shoot Argos summer commercials on 3 July?' No, is the short and long answer to that. The only way it can be done is if they come out to Jo'burg and shoot all day Sunday the 4th on my day off. Glad I'm not the person having to relay this to Argos.

Alex Oakley's addition to tomorrow's call sheet cheers me up:

COMPTON HOUSE. MASTER BEDROOM.
*Ruby and Harry finish cross-dressing. Ralph asks Harry to wear pink.*

### *19 June 2004*

All day shooting interior dining-room scenes. Blackouts make the cramped room very hot. With only three characters, all seated, there is a limit to ways in which to shoot them, yet despite having done similar set-ups in the past two weeks, Pierre's problems with eye-lines remain, as he wants actors to play to a mark on the side of the camera, but Emily Watson has refused to do scenes where she is unable to look directly at the actor she is playing opposite. I ask Charlie and Karen if they are prepared to convene a meeting with Pierre and the French production manager tomorrow evening to try and sort this out once and for all. If we need to get him a camera operator, we have to do so *now*. It's got to the point where I feel unable to ask for any tracking shots as they seem to cause him major headaches and prompt endless cursing.

# SHOOTING

## 20 June 2004

Day off. Zoomed down to Mbabane to see the progress of the Theatre Club sets for *Camelot*. Gary's art-department crew is supplemented by very enthusiastic amateur volunteers. They remind me of how I loved doing anything and everything I could in the theatre during my adolescence. Even though most of the people who created this club in the early sixties are now dead or gone and it's in a pretty parlous state, every corner of it is familiar and welcoming and it's a total pleasure to be back to recreate and revisit its past.

Spent the rest of the afternoon alone – relief, after being with so many people every minute of the day and night.

Returned to Pigg's Peak for the 7 p.m. meeting in the hotel boardroom with Pierre et al. When the technical eye-line issues are raised and he is asked if he needs an operator – as he had when working on *Monsieur N.* – he storms out shouting. Charlie and Karen are unequivocal in their views about how slow we are working and they firmly believe that we need to get a camera operator on board. This is vetoed outright by MC.

After an hour, Pierre reappears and lays all blame at my door, saying that I have been distant and uninvolved with him. It sounds like a marital spat and I try my best to reassure him that having spent so much time together on the recces agreeing on how *every* scene will be shot, my attention during the actual filming *has* to be on the actors. I apologize for 'neglecting him' and failing 'to pay him enough attention'. I reiterate that I am thrilled with the first rushes we have seen and that his cinematography is stunning. I remind him that during the utter chaos of pre-production, which he witnessed first hand, I had assumed we were sufficiently comfortable with each other *not* to have to keep stroking egos all the time.

And I was worried that the actors would be the divas . . .

I suggest that we all meet in the bar after work every evening and that the French camera crew don't automatically go to dinner as a separate group. They say, 'But it's a relief for us not to have to speak English – that is why we like to eat by ourselves.' Resolutions are tabled: I will collaborate with and reassure the French camera crew *daily*; Pierre and Karen are not to argue about eye-lines in front of the actors; Pierre agrees to control his swearing, and reassures us that he is capable of lighting as well as operating. We all repair to the bar for a jar and some bonhomie, and I resolve to meet Pierre at breakfast every day and go through the day ahead so that we are all clear about how, what, where and why.

### *21 June 2004*

Am *very* vigilant and solicitous of our hitherto neglected French brothers and sisters in the camera and sound departments. Everything is more efficient so the fraught meeting, painful though it was, has paid dividends.

Breakfast scene with Gabriel, Emily and Nick. After the drunken night of bottles being thrown and doors slammed, the characters are filled with remorse and unspoken recrimination. I ask that none of the actors look each other in the eye. Gabriel suggests that he drink a full tumbler of water as alcoholics get so dehydrated. In this small detail, he subtly transforms something straightforward on the page into something painful and desperate on screen. Chrissie Baker has added a shaving cut on his chin to imply that the morning after has begun rough.

However, Gabriel's unique relationship with inanimate objects is such that Karen is kept busy reminding him with which hand he grabs his napkin or glass, in what order and when. Between set-ups he tells epic anecdotes that have everyone crippled with laughter, only to plunge into the most soul-searching details about the scene in hand.

Emily's unwavering sense of authenticity is acutely evident in take after take of her breaking down in tears, realizing that her new husband is a chronic drunk. Her instinct is perfectly pitched throughout, and I know how gruelling it is to do these kinds of scenes repeatedly. The set is noticeably quieter whenever she is working and her face is such that you want to 'rest' in it. An unalloyed joy to work with.

### 22 June 2004

Another efficient, calm day. We shoot the post-Independence ceremony scene on the veranda when Gabriel's arm becomes paralysed and he drops a teacup. This is a pivotal moment presaging his death, filmed in slow motion and at normal speed. Oli and Graham, our props maestros, have a total of six duplicate cups to shoot with, so no pressure there then, Gabriel! Only he could do a take in which his paralysed arm goes *up* instead of down. Fifth take: arm, teacup, crash are in perfect sync.

Alex Oakley informs me that no payments have been made yet to the actors, and even the contracts remain unsigned. Alex has good news, though – MC is flying back to France for a week.

Kathy Lette, my novelist friend in London, emails to say that she met Miranda Richardson at a party and she was positively raving about her first week of filming, which is balm to my ears. *And* Julie Walters is due to arrive soon. Hurrah!

### 23 June 2004

Two long drunk scenes scheduled. Gabriel is concerned that these drink-fuelled tirades be significantly different and clearly motivated, worried about being too unsympathetic. The necessity of having to shoot both on the same day is not ideal, but it forces us to examine how to make the degrees of his drunkenness different. Emily comes up trumps by reassuring Gabriel that these explosions are best seen as part of this family's routine. He launches into the 'dark side' with total conviction. For me this reiterates the fact that, despite my father's most extreme drunken furies, I never stopped loving him – I just loathed the demon that the drink unleashed.

Nick and Emily give their all, even though they are mostly reacting off camera to him. Gabriel is hugely appreciative of their concentration, as am I. I remember how dispiriting it was to do scenes 'opposite' Bruce Willis in *Hudson Hawk* – reacting to *his* dialogue, but when the camera was reversed onto me, he was mostly absent and I would have to speak to a camera mark, his lines read by the female script supervisor.

The re-enactment of my father's outbursts and my complete involvement directing and watching the scene on the monitor prompt Martin Jaubert to ask Karen Jones if I am all right – 'He is very intense, no?' I suspect this is a euphemism for 'Is the director barking mad?'

Despite the relentless schedule pressure, Gabriel is triumphant today and the respect he garners from the crew is palpable and verbalized. He tells Emily that he is having the best working experience of his life making this film. Which makes my day.

Alex Oakley's call sheet demands that 'tomorrow will be a loud/unpleasant shirt day – the prize will be a wonderfully crafted elephant in real pine.'

Phone home and very worried to hear that our daughter is vomiting all the time and the doctor says her immune system is very low. I feel impotent and frustrated at being so far away.

## 24 June 2004

Feels like a holiday – the study scene of reconciliation between father and son is so simply played and touching, and technically relatively straightforward, that we get ahead of schedule. Nick dabbles with red sealing wax during his dialogue with Gabriel, and the smell of the burning wax is such an instant and powerful throwback, I feel as though my late father could walk through the door at any moment.

The next big scene back in the blacked-out drawing room revolves around the 'drunken' return of Harry, who is actually sober, and who reveals he has just been asked to stay on as an honorary adviser after Independence. Gabriel had been obsessing about how to do this and suggests that he go really over the top, pretending to be legless, before 'sobering up' instantaneously to confess his good news. Works a treat, and the combination of big, bad loud-shirt day and the upbeat nature of the scenes convinces us that Portugal don't stand a chance of winning the football this evening.

Sid and Nick are poised and primed for a great victory in the bar, everyone cheering England on. Portugal win on penalties.

Distracted by the 10.15 p.m. arrival of three days' worth of rushes. Everyone funnels down the stairwell to the basement and watches the marathon of footage on the small TV screen. Very encouraging and compliments all round.

## 25 June 2004

Another location move, another military manoeuvre. The roads are steep and our start gets delayed as the main lighting truck breaks down en route.

The Highland Inn, the first hotel in the country, built at the turn of the last century when there was a mini-gold-rush in Pigg's Peak, is being used as a hospital set. Gary has painted the corridor walls utility green and redressed the reception room with a portrait of the Queen and a Bakelite telephone. Oli, Graham and Flo Ballack have worked their art and prop department magic.

First day with a new character – John Matshikiza, playing Dr Mzimba. I knew John briefly when he was living in self-imposed exile in London in the eighties, working at the RSC and the National. He returned to South Africa after Mandela's release, writes a column for a Jo'burg newspaper and does very little acting now. He's somewhat cautious coming onto a set where everyone has had two weeks to get to know one another.

I emphasize that he and Gabriel portray a friendship of equals, and avoid the patronizing cliché of African and European friendships in so many films – which my father referred to as 'bending over black-wards'. These are two educated men who have known each other all their adult lives, with a shared ironic overview and cynical sense of humour. Somehow this has to convey itself in very short scenes.

The scene in which Dr Mzimba tells Emily and Nick that Gabriel has only weeks to live is acted with stunned outward calm. No histrionics, making it all the more devastating.

The day we told my father that he was terminally ill with cancer is something I have regretted ever since. Although he'd been hospitalized to have a brain tumour removed, he had clearly never computed that he might only have months left to live. The subsequent nightmare of having a lung removed, the resurgence of further brain tumours and his inability to speak was a gruesome downward spiral as he gradually shrivelled and withered away. By the time he died, he had aged from looking like what he was, a fifty-two-year-old man, to an octogenarian in Belsen.

### *26 June 2004*

Spend the entire day shooting a two-minute scene which has no dialogue, effectively a ballet of tracking shots detailing the preparation for Gabriel's brain-tumour operation to a playback of a profoundly melancholy Chopin prelude, played via an iPod and speakers.

The extras drafted in to play nurses and surgical assistants are very keen to do everything just right and the combination of the music, fluid back and forth movements, transferring Gabriel from bed to stretcher, injecting his arm, shaving his head and trolleying him out to the operating theatre worked like clockwork after detailed rehearsals.

I wrote this sequence to be heightened and unrealistic, to give this crucial moment a dignity that was denied my dad when he actually underwent all this. It is an unequivocally emotional scene and I felt very fragile and raw all day. As did Emily – who lost her great friend Katrin Cartlidge, with whom she did *Breaking the Waves*, who died so tragically and prematurely in 2002 at the age of forty-one.

Gabriel's bandaged head looks uncannily like my father's from a certain angle when he is lying down. Playing the Chopin helps sustain the mood of the scene and the crew are wonderfully respectful towards the actors, especially Emily and Nick, who spend an exhausting day in tears.

During the running buffet-lunch break – everyone standing

rather than sitting down in order to get the day's work completed due to the late start and fading winter light – Julie Walters and Julian Wadham arrive to meet, greet and eat. I have known them both for years, and I can't quite get my head around seeing them at the Highlands Inn of all places!

Julie is a conundrum – at once the most approachable, genuinely funny and accessible person you could ever wish to meet, yet intensely private and at some level totally unknowable. Julian is unabashedly, unapologetically public-school charm itself. He makes no attempt to 'mockney' his accent or disguise his background in any way and he is perfect casting as Charles. They have heard about the rushes already and claim to feel 'nervy' about getting started as the benchmark has been set 'so high'. Thrilled to hear this!

We've completed the first three weeks of shooting *on* schedule *without* dropping a single scene. The art department have organized a barbecue at their rented house with Bob the medic in charge of the cooking, to which everyone is invited – including Fenella Woolgar, who has just arrived and clearly feeling fish-out-of-water unfamiliar. The house is above the Phophonyane waterfall, and although freezing cold, the star-filled night sky is so breathtaking that most people brave the outdoors in blankets and coats. Drumming, dancing, boozing and burnt food round off a great week, with the prospect of a free Sunday tomorrow, which people are planning as if it were a week's holiday. The advantage of all being isolated in a single location for the first few weeks is that it welds everyone together in a way that never happens in a city.

### 27 June 2004

Hysterical day with Julie Walters, Fenella Woolgar and Karen 'Gin' Jones (on account of her penchant for a relaxing G&T after work) driving through the southern section of the Kruger Game Park across the border in South Africa. Julie keeps up a running commentary on all the animals, providing them with funny voices and a variety of accents: elephants from *Acorn Antiques*, Brummie baboons, Irish warthogs, Lancastrian giraffes, Cockney crocodiles and so on. There is a slight undertow of hysteria as we are all so far from home and our respective families. When I asked how they saw themselves in old age, the response was unanimous – in the countryside surrounded by animals.

### *28 June 2004*

All day shooting in the drawing room, but at least most of the work is in daylight, so it's not so hot and claustrophobic. First day for Julian, and we allow extra time for him to feel comfortable and part of it all.

One long scene is shot with the camera tracking Emily as she moves back and forth around the room, which is a challenge for the focus puller and camera operator as it takes forever to set up and rehearse. Everything has to work in one go, and it requires sixteen takes.

A single, long take like this is the nearest equivalent to doing a play, and I think this makes Julian's first day of work 'easier' in that the scene is not chopped up into little sections which requires a different sort of concentration. Much more satisfying, and he seems pleased by the end of it. As am I.

I'm even happier at the prospect of seeing my wife and daughter, who are flying out from London tonight and will be here tomorrow afternoon.

## 29 June 2004

The call sheet emphatically states *No visitors are allowed on set without prior permission of the producers*. Given that there isn't a producer in the country, let alone on the set, this becomes a running gag.

First day's shooting for Fenella, who is starting with her biggest scene in the film, first up, playing June. She's worried that she doesn't just play a braying Hooray cliché. As with Julian, I recognize that playing a supporting role requires an inverse proportion of attention, encouragement and support – the leads have endless scenes in which to display their various feathers, whereas a supporting actor comes in cold, pressured to make a mark and establish a three-dimensional character in a much shorter time.

Fenella is *highly* self-critical, so it takes many takes before she feels she has cracked her first entrance. As she's so bright and perceptive, it's hugely enjoyable to watch her play someone so thick and insensitive. Her scripted clash with Julie Walters, as they both vie for Gabriel's attentions, is an unbridled delight. I can't think of another actor who can convey the volume of pain that Julie does when patronized by someone supposedly higher up the social ladder. It is the combination of hurt and defiance in her narrowed eyes that is simultaneously funny and moving, something that has characterized her work ever since her screen breakthrough in *Educating Rita*.

My wife and daughter appear mid-afternoon, and having so longed and looked forward to their arrival, I am completely discombobulated when I see them casually wander up through the garden. Went round the corner and three of us hugged and held onto one another to bursting. My family, my stays, my compass, my east, west, north and south, my everything worth living and loving for.

An almighty thunderstorm in the evening and an electric-power failure. Urgent calls to the weather centre to determine tomorrow's conditions as we are scheduled to shoot Gabriel's funeral.

### 1 July 2004

*'Crew – please wear long trousers, sturdy boots and long-sleeved tops at this location, to avoid tick bites.'*

Mountainside burial scene. Sunny-skyed. Sixty extras are drafted in as mourners, giving the make-up, wig and wardrobe teams their biggest test so far. The sky and valley below look as if they've been vacuumed by the night storm, and it's the clearest it's been since we started filming. Chrissie Baker is convinced that I have a guardian angel hovering over me. Although a non-believer, I am ready to bow my head to *any* deity for the perfect weather this morning.

After detailing all the various shots and set-ups with the camera crew after breakfast, actually seeing the properly dug grave on the mountainside proved overwhelming. Whilst the cast and extras were being readied, I drove back to the hotel and woke my wife up saying that I'd lost my nerve and couldn't do it. I didn't know what to say to the extras, feeling inadequate and incapable of directing this scene. She talked me down, reminding me that when she did the dialect coaching on *Yentl*, Barbra Streisand was often afflicted by waves of self-doubt and would calm herself down with a simple 'one step at a time' mantra.

Drove back and brave-faced it, playing Abdullah Ibrahim's haunting and melancholic music to set the mood. The advantage of playing music on set is that it keeps everyone's volume level down and concentration up. The only other time I have worked like this was on *Dracula*, where Francis Ford Coppola regularly played music to establish the appropriate atmosphere.

I explain the plan for the day and the choreography of where everyone stands, moves and exits. It's hard to control the emotions this conjures up, and I'm grateful when it's done. Seeing my daughter (cast to play Nick's girlfriend) standing at the graveside of the grandfather she never met made it all the more poignant, topped off by Mathokhoza's choir, dressed in traditional Swazi Mahiyas, singing funeral songs in Siswati.

John Carlisle, veteran actor from the RSC and the National, is here to play Sir Gifford Hardwick, the High Commissioner, and delivers his funeral oration at full welly. He is followed by Sibusiso Mamba, the first Swazi actor to graduate from RADA, playing Father Ndlovu.

As my father resolutely refused any religiosity in his life, there was no church service and his coffin was already in the open grave when the mourners arrived. He was fluent in Siswati and honoured with a Swazi name, Mathlaganipani – 'the man whose brain runs faster than his feet'. All his dying doubts about his true relationship with the Swazis he had known, befriended and worked with were laid to rest, for as far as you could see there were crowds of Swazi mourners, vastly outnumbering the British remnants of the colonial old guard. Like today, it was a brilliantly clear morning in a place that felt like the mountain top of the world. His great friend Pat Forsyth-Thompson gave an oration that charted his life (which John Carlisle repeats almost word for word), followed by an impromptu address from the young Father Ndlovu, fresh from an evangelical college in the US. What happened next was Monty Python meets Joe Orton: after an incredibly emotive speech he suddenly leapt into the open grave and began unscrewing the coffin, chanting in a near trance that he was 'GOING TO RAAAAAISE THE DEAD, I AM GOING TO RAAAAAAAISE MATHLAGANIPANI FROM THE DEAD!' Nobody knew what to do; people surged forward to see what was going on, my stepmother staggered sideways, and within no time he had the lid off and was commanding and beseeching that his faith and power resurrect my dad. A terrible curiosity forced me to look down, to see what I did not want to see – the near-skeletal remnant of my pater, waxen and 'gone'. After I don't know how long, the priest began weeping and wailing uncontrollably, having failed to fulfil his evangelical quest for a miracle, and was hauled out of the grave and had to be consoled for what he felt was his 'failure of faith'.

Sibusiso gives it his all, for take after take. One of the extras confides that he was at my father's funeral and he takes some convincing that, bizarre as it was, it would have made my father laugh, and he would have loved to have seen how many people turned out for his 'leaving'.

An appropriately ancient Swazi man shuffles past Nick as scripted, and hands him a crumpled note reading 'Goodbye Baba Mathlaganipani – do not forget us'. In reality, I only got to read this note at the lunch after the funeral, but the inversion of the usual 'we will never forget you' precisely pinpointed the feeling of having been left behind among the living. Death had somehow been given the aspect of a destination to which we were all denied entry. I had held it together during the actual funeral, but it was reading this simple, scrawled note that truly undid me.

Alex and Charlie report that the weather forecast for Monday is bad, which is when we are scheduled to shoot a barbecue that needs full sun. We swap it for Saturday, two days from now, though there is one *small* problem – Miranda Richardson, who appears halfway through the scene, is in London. Frantic phone around to locate and persuade her to come out earlier.

### 2 July 2004

Complete all the funeral close-ups in the morning, blessed by another day of blazing sunshine. Both Emily and Julie are incredibly poignant in their 'farewells', scattering handfuls of petals onto the coffin.

A much less stressful day in that the bulk of the work and control of the overall action has been completed, affording the luxury of time for the lead actors to get the close-up details just right. Nobody is bitten by ticks or snakes. After lunch, mini-location move back up to the house and the vegetable garden with Mathokoza Sibiyu, playing Dozen, singing his audition piece 'Onward, Christian Soldiers' for the *Camelot* music director, Bunny, played by Kim Borrell. It's a welcome relief to be doing such a funny and uplifting scene after the funeral.

Kim is an amateur actress with whom I did plays at school, and it's a real treat to be able to have her on board, as it is having Sindi Nxumalo, whom I have also known since way back when, play the housekeeper Regina.

Relief to hear that Miranda has boarded her flight in London; relief also that the funeral scenes are completed and that having almost lost my nerve, nobody noticed.

### 3 July 2004

Julian Wadham's big day, the scene where, during Ruby's 4th of July barbecue party, he suggests producing an amateur production of *Camelot* as a 'cultural swansong to the Swazi people' to celebrate Independence and impress Princess Margaret. Gabriel expressed concerns that as there are so few scenes where he and Emily are *not* at war due to the demon drink, this is the perfect opportunity for his character to make a welcome speech to all their friends, *before* Julian cajoles them with *his* plans. Practically, this means that Gabriel writes himself a speech in which he publicly declares his love for Ruby and welcomes everyone – meaning that Julian's 'thunder' is somewhat hijacked, as he is meant to open proceedings and dominate.

# SHOOTING

This is a hard call for me – having done so many rewrites over the years to reduce and make each scene as tight as I possibly can, the idea that it needs expanding is anathema. However, the collaborative way in which the actors have worked has been so rewarding that I have to give them the benefit of my unspoken doubt and run with it.

This scene is a concertina of actual events that took place years apart – Independence took place in 1968, presided over by Princess Alexandra, and the Theatre Club mounted *Free as Air* for the celebrations. *Camelot* was done in 1975 and Princess Margaret attended *The Merchant of Venice* in 1980, leaving at the interval. My script has amalgamated these various events so that Independence takes place in 1971, and *Camelot* is the show chosen to impress Princess Margaret, who leaves halfway through.

Miranda arrives safe and sound in time to film her entrance after lunch. Julian/Charles delivers his *Camelot* plans with supreme charm and conviction, Gabriel/Harry expresses the pride and joy of a man newly in love again, Julie/Gwen levitates at the prospect of doing a show and meeting a royal, whilst Miranda/Lauren interrupts proceedings with her icy arrival and removal of Nick/Ralph.

Jane Stephens has invited the entire unit to a 'farewell Boshimela' party at her house this evening, which I am heart-sore to be missing as I have to drive four hours to Jo'burg to do the Argos commercial tomorrow, Argos payments being the financial saviour during the past non-paying years of rewrites and trying to get the film off the ground. Film-unit driver Hodges Sibeko kindly drives, affording me the luxury of sleeping the whole journey on the back seat after an utterly exhausting week. Check into the hotel at midnight.

*4 July 2004*

Director Paul Weilland and co-star Julia Sawalha relentlessly tease and remind me what a great favour they are doing by flying halfway across the world to accommodate me. It's utterly bizarre to be a hired hand again in the midst of directing my own flick. I sit in make-up having my rock-and-roll wig fitted, free of any pressures, decisions or technical demands for the day. The location is a Nigerian mobile-phone squillionaire's mansion that he occupies for six days a year, a high-walled, maximum-security Spanish-style palace. Oh, the ironies of Africa . . .

This being a commercial, it's a rude reminder that we have the 'luxury' of doing seventy-nine takes (I wish I was kidding) of my getting a hamburger out of an Argos fridge that supposedly belonged to Elvis. Well, that's the gag. Totally surreal – the cost of flying every-one out here, the mansion, my day off, the advert, the number of takes, being in the murder capital of the world, hearing that Paul's own film has gone into 'turnaround' because Billy Bob Thornton has pulled out, driving back to Pigg's Peak in the evening to storyboard the deathbed scenes of my father for tomorrow. Paul is very gener-ous and encouraging about my film, concluding that making a low-budget flick is like a much loved hobby at best – done for the love of it – as you are guaranteed to be financially shafted!

He generously lets me go by 5.30 p.m., so that I will not be comatose for tomorrow's shoot. Get back to Pigg's Peak at 10 p.m. and the call sheet makes me laugh:

Lost property – *Natori* padded bra, pink, 32B. Please come and claim.

# SHOOTING

## *5 July 2004*

Everyone is raving about the amazing party given by Jane. The weather *has* turned, and the scene planned for the garden is relocated to the veranda where the light can be better controlled. Originally written to be a tender, silent scene between dying father and son, listening to *Round the Horne*, Gabriel and Emily have rightly suggested she be present, quietly filing his nails.

Gabriel is bandaged and made up to look gaunt and grey. We have two camera angles – one on Gabriel and Nick and the complementary reverse on Emily, all listening to the radio playback of Kenneth Williams, Hugh Paddick and Kenneth Horne performing their inimitable 'Julian and Sandy' routine. The takes are long and without dialogue, the actors conveying everything in their exchanged looks. What reads as a few descriptive lines in the script is transformed by their remarkable talent in simply listening and reacting. If it is anything like as poignant and moving in the finished film as it is to witness here, we will be home and not a dry eye in the house. To have a scene so perfectly realized is a pleasure more profound than any experience I have ever had being an actor for hire.

The next scene takes place in the drawing room, with Gabriel asleep on the sofa after his brain operation, surrounded by family and friends discussing their plans post-Independence. It is Celia Imrie's first day on the film, playing Lady Riva, who interrupts the scene by declaring that she 'doesn't do funerals'.

Celia had told me a story about her late mother, who had a habit of asking someone for directions and then dismissing them halfway through with imperious sang-froid. We incorporate this anecdote by having her say to Regina/Sindi, 'I say, could you tell me the way to—ooh, she'll never know.'

Although this is Celia's first day, it is Lady Riva's last scene. Celia plays it at full imperious pomp, having mined me for anything and everything she can about the woman it is based upon. She commits to it with the energy and conviction of playing the lead. Celia is one of life's great enhancers, who thrills at the adventure of it all and could not be a more welcome arrival if she'd tried. She can barely contain her excitement at being in Africa for the first time, and having worked with both Julie, Emily and me before, is in familiar company.

The deathbed scene in the master bedroom between father and son proves very emotional to revisit. The film version is visually far less gruesome than the reality. My father's illness lasted nine months from diagnosis to his death. This is heavily truncated for the film, and based on the man in the ward next to him who had galloping cancer which killed him in six weeks.

The last coherent words my father ever spoke to me were, 'I never stopped loving your mother.' He eked this out when my stepmother briefly left the room. I was so shocked I asked *which* mother he meant – pointing at the door – and he repeated, '*Your* mother.' Despite his impeded speech due to the multiple brain tumours that grew after one cruelly brief month of remission, he was at pains to impart this to me. There was no mistaking what he had uttered, and it felt like a bomb going off in my face. This was a confession from a man who had not had any direct contact with my mother for years, and yet it made sense of everything. In that instant I understood the tragedy of his life – unrequited love, the pain of which no amount of alcohol could ever quite numb. No amount of love from my stepmother could ever quite suffice. It was as cruel, true and sad a sentence as any I'd ever heard or read.

Having discussed this at length and in depth with Gabriel in advance, I don't dare presume trying to 'direct' him in any specific way, this being a moment that belongs simultaneously to Gabriel and my father. When he whispers the words, they are charged with the most gut-wrenching emotion. There's nothing for me to say, other than to thank him for his total commitment and understanding of this role.

Young as he is, Nick Hoult responds to this 'revelation' with the utmost sincerity, and the bond he and Gabriel have developed socially and working together so intensely these past four weeks is evident in how they act together.

We shoot Emily/Ruby returning to the room after this private confession, sitting on the bed and taking Gabriel's hand. I suspect that this scene might seem like a betrayal, but we have it as an option in the editing in the months ahead.

With Gabriel/Harry now dead, all that remains is to film the bedroom, empty except for the wheelchair, some bedclothes and Nick/Ralph looking around, finding his father's cricket jumper and inhaling the smell of it.

All this is filmed in the bedroom of Jane's father, Bob, who died a year ago at the age of ninety-six, and who knew my father very well. I could not bring myself to keep any of my father's clothes or shoes, but I have his watch, pith helmet, ceremonial sword and OBE as keepsakes, all of which are used as props in the film.

### 6 July 2004

Weather report for our last day at Boshimela: 'Cold, bleak with heavy cloud cover all day. 30% chance of rain. Maximum temperature 14ºC.'

Our farewell lunch in the marquee is topped off by the surprise arrival of all the Swazi women who work at Boshimela in the mohair-weaving studios adjacent to the house, singing us off on our way, led by the beautiful and inimitable Bebee Shongwe. Many people are crying; everyone is clapping and cheering. I'm given a very long-legged wooden sculpture of 'myself' replete with purple trousers, red jacket, beads and a white face with Swazi features. We all form a circle outside, wherein various celebrants dance a solo, ranging from a six-year-old 'warrior' to Mathokoza, to ladies well into their sixties. It is the most perfect farewell 'gift' for our time here in Pigg's Peak.

While we have broken the back of the film, it is with real regret that the intimacy of shooting at Boshimela is now over. At wrap, there is a mass scramble to get luggage loaded up, bills paid and minivan off to the Ezulweni Valley, south of Mbabane, two hours' drive away.

Hold on tight saying goodbye to Jane, for being so accommodating and generous – letting us invade her family home en masse, through all the stops and false starts during the past three years. Neither of us can quite believe it's actually happened.

Feel like real country bumpkins checking into the Royal Swazi Hotel after Pigg's Peak, and invite the entire cast for dinner at the Calabash restaurant, sensing that most people will be discombobulated after the intimate familiarity of the past month at Boshimela. It gives me an opportunity to socialize with the actors who have not been working every day, like Sid, Fenella, Julian, John and Miranda.

Alex Oakley is advised to fly back to London with suspected tick-bite fever, having spent all night vomiting. *Very* sad to see him go, as he has been the most upbeat and no-shit-Sherlock second assistant director you could wish for. Adriaan Van Zyl, our stalwart production secretary, has to leave as well because his mother is ill. Reel life/*real* life.

We decide to get Andrew McEwan back out from England to replace Alex. Mercifully he is free and, having brought out the wigs and costumes at the eleventh hour the day before we started shooting, knows everyone.

Directing, like hosting a party, means that you're essentially on the outside, always looking in, hoping to keep everything and everyone looked after and attended to properly. Despite being surrounded by people and constantly bombarded with questions, always on call

and required to make choices and decisions, it feels curiously isolat-
ing. Every now and again I long just to sit around between set-ups
and yak with the actors. But the rewards of writing and directing the
whole shebang are enormous.

## 7 July 2004

First set of the day is literally through the front doors of the Royal
Swazi Hotel, standing in for the grand entrance to Government
House. Gary and his team have erected false posts, sentry boxes,
wrought-iron gates and two guards to pomp up the colonial nature
of the OBE ceremonials. As it's midweek and 6.30 a.m., and most of
the crew have gone ahead to the Mantenga Bridge location ten
minutes' drive away to prep for the next scene, there are very few
people about and the shots are done relatively quickly.

It's somewhat weird to be staying in this hotel, having worked
here during my university holidays as a junior public-relations
skivvy in the mid-seventies, when the hotel casino attracted hordes
of tourists from South Africa, where gambling was illegal. Despite
the immense wealth of some of the regular clientele, I was given the
entertaining but unenviable task of stopping certain guests at the
desk to check out their luggage, housekeeping having alerted reception to the fact that towels, bathrobes and ashtrays were missing.
Without fail, the noisier the protests – 'Don't you know who I am?
Do you have any idea how much I'm worth?' – the likelier it was
that they had stolen everything they could. I would reply with the
panto pretence of 'I'm quite sure there has been some mistake, sir,
it won't take me a minute to remove the misplaced items, madam,
so sorry to have troubled you.' The wives were the worst and invari-
ably spat through their dentures that they would 'never set foot in
this place ever again', only to be seen the following weekend. Either

they suffered from early Alzheimer's, gambler's rot or short-term memory loss or it was just plain bald-faced shamelessness.

The gift shop used to be a hairdressing salon presided over by one Paul-Henry, the only gay in this colonial village. He wore his hair in a mauve Quentin Crisp-ish pompadour, and sported long fingernails and those blouson shirts favoured by ice skaters and ballroom dancers. He looked and spoke like nobody else in Swaziland, and was adored and fiercely protected by his female clients, whilst feared and reviled by their husbands. 'Bats for the other side' was as far as most explanations went when kids asked any whys and wherefores. When my father began to take my acting ambitions more seriously, Paul-Henry hovered like some spectral warning of what he suspected the acting profession would be like – 'Bit of a queer bunch, if you ask me.'

The old iron Mantenga Bridge was built by the British in 1948 and is located below Execution Rock, from which nineteenth-century wrongdoers were legendarily flung to their deaths – the perfect setting for Ralph to hear some momentous revelations from his mother, Lauren.

Miranda expertly manoeuvres her Mini Cooper to a screeching halt, fumbles for a cigarette and slams out of the car, furious at having just been snubbed by Lady Riva and June at the Mahlanya vegetable market – a scene we have yet to shoot. She is resolutely unsympathetic in her rage and doesn't give a damn about being liked or lovable. Her volcanics are Bette Davis-like in ferocity, and magnificent to watch, ruthless yet vulnerable. After each take she is dismissive of praise and diverts attention from herself by being flippant and nonchalant, before turning it on again with undiluted power for the next take.

A common misconception about actors is that they are a vainglorious tribe. My experience is that compliments are oddly embarrassing. The *idea* of being admired and yodelled at by total strangers might seem appealing, but in reality leaves you feeling inadequate – a contradictory mixture of low self-esteem and large ego, hence the desire to disappear into someone else's shoes. Odd then to be praised for being someone you're not.

The contra-zoom, invented by Steven Spielberg, is a camera trick whereby the actors stand in a fixed position, with the camera tracking in towards them whilst the focus simultaneously zooms backwards, giving the surreal effect of them moving steadily apart when in fact they are standing still. Being a Techno-saurus I cannot properly explain this but I have asked Pierre to try and achieve it as we're shooting a crucial moment of realization for Ralph, and I'm sure it's the way to heighten the moment. It takes a great deal of time to rehearse and get right technically, especially for the focus puller who has to be in perfect tandem with the camera operator and grip pushing the camera dolly. Requires twelve takes before everyone is satisfied.

The sun keeps going behind heavy clouds before coming out again, forcing us to shoot the whole scene in sun, then in cloud, then sun again, to try and avoid the editor's wrath and maintain visual continuity. I often think that this is when actors *really* earn their stripes, maintaining their concentration and readiness for whenever they hear – 'The light is good *now*!'

The French crew repeatedly express their admiration for the English actors' discipline – for knowing their lines, being fully prepared and able to hit their designated camera marks on each take. When they describe working with French actors, one word springs from their lips: 'Cha-o-tic.' They are especially impressed with Zac Fox, as are we all, because he has grasped the technical aspects effortlessly, finding his key light and camera marks without sacrificing anything of his performance.

Editor Isabelle Dedieu is here for a two-day surprise visit and enthuses about the rushes, how wonderful it all looks, how strong the performances are, that I am 'a natural director'. Thrilled to hear this, of course, but also embarrassed. (See three paragraphs back!)

*Camelot* singing rehearsals are held in a corner of the hotel lounge before dinner. Sid Mitchell, having revealed that he is a trained hoofer, becomes our surprise 'choreographer'! Likewise Fenella, having claimed not to play the piano very well, hits the ivories like a seasoned pro. The desultory guests floating past aren't quite sure if we are the restaurant cabaret rehearsing in mufti, or a long-lost am-dram troupe from the last century.

Rushes of the hospital scenes arrive, and everyone crams into an unused bedroom to watch them on the TV. They are everything I'd hoped for, and more: fluid, clear and charged with emotion. This boosts our morale hugely.

### 8 July 2004

All hands on deck lighting and prepping the marquee set up in the hotel gardens for the OBE ceremony. Rehearsing the Steadicam shot following Gabriel, Miranda and Zac down the curving staircase into the garden and entering the pomp and tatty splendour of the tent takes up most of the morning. At lunchtime I'm panicked that we will run out of time.

John Carlisle and Celia Imrie give it the full imperial welly as Sir Gifford and Lady Riva, his wife, with all the hauteur and self-possession of Catherine the Great. John has a combination of old-style charm and a roué's roving eye, whilst Celia has determined that Lady Riva has *also* put herself about, and invests the simple act of attaching the OBE medal to Gabriel's chest with territorial sexual innuendo.

A troop of vervet monkeys arrive on the roof to inspect the action and we try to bribe them with bananas to get them into the background, to no avail.

Gabriel comes up with the idea of forcibly smooching Miranda full on the mouth, in full view of everyone and for far too long, just after he has accepted his medal, instead of the tame kiss as scripted. This is a pointedly public display of possession, knowing as he does that all the assembled guests are aware she is having an affair with his former best friend John Traherne, played by Ian Roberts, here with his wife Gwen/Julie Walters.

This is followed by a handshake of congratulation from Traherne, scripted to be perfunctory, but Gabriel suggests he *grip* his opponent's hand for an inordinately long time, empowering himself publicly and very passionately. I notice that Gabriel and Ian have not spent any time together – is life imitating art . . . ?

Again and again I realize how indebted I am to the actors' talent for imbuing and investing a character with so much more than is simply conveyed on the page.

Andrew McEwan, our new second assistant director, is here, thrown in at the deep end with so many actors and extras to deal with on his first day. No one has yet been able to diagnose precisely what is wrong with Alex Oakley, who is undergoing further tests in London.

During a lighting break, Charlie talks me through the schedule for the week ahead and my brain goes into a tailspin of panic that we will never get everything done, but I resolve to try for some outward calm.

Julie Walters' daughter Maisie, Karen Jones' daughters Robyn and Jess and Celia Imrie's son Angus have all arrived – the palpable relief of reunited families makes for a happier set.

The art department are chasing their own tails, no sooner finishing one set than they have to have the vegetable market prepped for tomorrow, followed by disguising a side road to make it look like it's 1971, and dressing the exterior of the Theatre Club. Likewise the costume, make-up, wigs and hair departments are facing a week of large numbers of extras and pre-dawn calls. They are the first to arrive at work and last to leave. I am astonished they never seem to have any complaints.

The advance schedule for the Theatre Club scenes reads like a Clapham Junction station timetable. Given a medium budget, it'd be spread over a couple of weeks; ours is shoehorned into six and a half days. Transport chief Sean Berkhout and location manager Jean-Roux Viljoen have to ensure that their convoy of vehicles gets to all three locations tomorrow. Their gung-ho attitude is reassuring, especially as the trucks have to negotiate the notorious Malegwane Hill – a three-thousand-foot climb from the Ezulweni Valley up to the capital, Mbabane. It used to have a skull-and-crossbones billboard stating how many people had been killed that year, with a staggering death toll.

*9 July 2004*

Location 1. Mahlanya market, Malkerns
Location 2. Dzeliwe Street, Mbabane
Location 3. Theatre Club, Msakato Street, Mbabane

Charlie Watson is in full military mode, determined to keep everything moving at full pelt. His mission is to prove that the insane schedule can be achieved; in this he is nothing short of zealous, and is not taking *any* prisoners or excuses. There is zero contingency for bad weather, vehicle breakdown, traffic jams or police roadblocks. It is a real measure of Lynne-Anne's and Toni's preparations that we have managed to arrive at these new locations, in a country where a film has never been made before, and get on with the work unobstructed by red tape or council restrictions, or any of the myriad bureaucratic nightmares that usually face any film production. I owe them both big time!

Mahlanya vegetable market is also a combination roadside bus stop, general store and local meeting point. All the market traders have agreed to play themselves for the morning and are completely laid back and accommodating of our invasion. The scene involves Lady Riva speaking to Ralph whilst blanking Lauren, recreating a scenario I suspect is familiar to most children of divorced parents – being spoken to by an adult friend of one parent, who simultaneously ignores the disfavoured parent who is present, putting the child in a 'piggy in the middle' position. This left me feeling angry *and* guilty: angered by the rude cruelty of it and guilty that I was spoken to whilst my mother was so patently ignored.

The actors' acute concentration means we conclude the scene by lunchtime, and the whole crew drive north to Mbabane.

A twenty-four-hour vomit-and-squit virus has hit – Karen Jones, Miranda Richardson, Ashley the make-up artist, Sid Mitchell, Zac Fox and Bob the medic have all succumbed.

When we get to the street location we find that the shop windows reflect all the crew and camera and lighting gubbins, so they have to be redressed immediately with flags and bunting, period cars and extras. A regiment of dancing, chanting royal warriors is preceded by a platoon of bare-breasted women in full traditional gear, signalling the imminence of Independence. During the set up, a crowd of onlookers have gathered around, and a familiar voice says hello to me out of a near-unrecognizable face I haven't seen in thirty years. This old school friend is now grey, balding, divorced and very grown up; the 'ghost' of who I knew back then hovers throughout our brief chat.

The Swazi warrior and maiden euphorics are watched by Lady Riva and June, both scripted to register disapproval that the end of Empire is nigh. However, Celia's decision to play Lady Riva as a predatory goer results in her initial disapproval giving way to a hormonal gear change, as she nostril-flares and eagerly follows the half-naked regiment. Nick and Sid follow in her wake, imitating her mercilessly.

The last location is only a short distance away but the light is fading and we only just manage to film Nick and Sid's entrance into the Theatre Club, which has been dressed with a castle facade, fairy lights and *Camelot* banner. This had been designed and painted by Tom Bayly, the local architect who directed the original *Camelot* production in 1975. He was a real mentor, generously lending from his large collection of plays, records and theatre magazines, providing me with a real education before I went to drama school. We have been great friends for thirty-three years and it's an odd role reversal, having been his amateur protégé but now returning as a professional writer/director and calling the shots.

The art department are buckling with the pressure and the foyer is not yet dressed for tomorrow's invasion, due to an alleged 'lapse' in negotiations between the Club committee and Lynne-Anne. We had contracted to spend a week in the clubhouse and theatre, but it's claimed that the members thought we would only move in on the *actual* day of shooting, with no prep time the night before. Hostility and resentment about our presence has been brewing for a while, the reasons for which no one can quite understand. Especially since the Club has deteriorated into little more than a drinking den for a substantially reduced membership of fifty, precious few of whom have any interest in the decrepit theatre itself, which stands to be repainted, repaired and rejuvenated at our expense and with the employment of over a hundred extras, plus an agreed rental fee. Some members see this as a real godsend, but one particularly obstructive martinet declares that it cannot be dressed yet as there is a private party booked in for the evening. Seems little more than a ruse to squeeze us for more money.

Fucking infuriating – he has known for weeks when we are due and it takes an exchange of cash to get him to postpone their do. It's ironic that the location which ought to be the *most* accommodating proves to be the most difficult. *Really* sticks in my craw, but then the petty internecine wars of committee members has ever been thus. It serves to remind how smoothly *everything* else has gone so far. In order to try and win over the chief obstructor, I ask if he would like to be a featured extra. He gladly accepts, then immediately argues with Lynne-Anne about his fee, claiming he 'usually gets paid *more* for extra work'. Bonkers – no film has ever been made here before! I have known this bloke for years and he has always been apparently amenable face to face, but to everyone else on the crew has been a total arsehole. It's moments like this when you want your 'producer' to diplomatically step in, and ease and charm the problem away.

Having finally been given permission to go ahead, the art department work all night to get it completed. The cast rehearse *Camelot* songs and basic dance moves around the hotel lounge piano after wrap with great gusto. Crossed wires with the costume department who have inadvertently assumed we only need a *dozen* dinner jackets for the theatre audience of extras, rather than *sixty*, so panic phone-around to try and locate some in a town that no longer has social need for such trappings.

It's questionable whether Miranda is able to work tomorrow, her last day, given that she has been struck down with the virus. Make tentative contingency plan to shoot something else, but we don't have that much choice.

The month's shooting with the main cast in Pigg's Peak seems like a doddle in retrospect. Dinner alone with my family to escape the onslaught of questions, costume shortfalls, crew squits, permit problems and schedule pressures.

### 10 July 2004

Early morning frost and it's freezing in the unheated Theatre Club. However, being in one location for the coming week is a bonus, almost like being in a studio. Miranda is on the mend and *will* work today, as will Karen Jones. In order to shoot Miranda 'out', as it's her last acting day, all her scenes are crammed together out of order. However, our start time is seriously delayed as the virus has wild-fired through the cast and crew, resulting in late arrivals and people laid off.

Spent the morning in the auditorium for a shot where Ralph sees *all* his parents in the stalls through a backstage spy-hole. The nego-tiating of which parent came to which performance was yet another piggy-in-the-middle scenario I remember all too acutely, wanting them both to come, but just not at the same time. The penalty of living in a colonial community was that everyone knew each other's business, and you couldn't move without someone having an opin-ion about it. The perfect dress rehearsal for living in Hollywood, and precisely the reason I subsequently embraced the anonymity of London.

The social stigma of divorce at that time meant that our family was subject to the kind of scrutiny and gossip which made me very self-conscious and suspicious of people's motives. This was an inadvertent precursor of fame, the conundrum of which is that whilst wanting recognition for your work, you recoil when your private self or life is derided.

It's a delightful bonus to have Julie, Karen, Celia, Chrissie and Gary's children as extras in this scene. The recreation of the bar décor circa 1971, replete with extras in late-sixties and early seven-ties dresses, is a real time warp. Some of the questions I get asked by the actors make me feel as if I grew up in the provincial dark ages, which doubtless I did. Small-town life is comfortably familiar and reassuring in one sense, but I found it stultifying and claustro-phobic and could not wait to get out. I keep being asked if I could ever come back and live here, and much as I love being back, I love it more because I know I'm not here to stay. Yet the moment I feel depressed in London, my first impulse is to jump on a plane to Swaz, for a 'top-up'.

Miranda delivers a public dismissal of Ruby in front of the

silenced theatregoers with undiluted venom, in sharp contrast to her emotionally heartfelt farewell on wrap. She has given a performance that ruthlessly avoided any sentimentality whatsoever. Her trademark quick-release helium giggle is a welcome surprise to everyone who doesn't know her, after watching her being so 'tough'. I feel very sad that she is going.

It's also the last scene for Ian Roberts, playing John Traherne. Whilst Miranda and Emily have all the dialogue, he is stoical and keeps mum, salvaging a modicum of dignity in this most public humiliation, blanked by Sir Gifford, pursued by his ex-wife Gwen, and pointedly ignored by Ralph. I am indebted to him for agreeing to play this cameo of so few lines, but which required such a strong presence.

The extended shooting hours, location moves and six-day weeks, topped off by the viral epidemic, have laid everyone low. Get back to the hotel and bump into one of the production execs from Jo'burg, who jauntily observes, 'Hasn't it all gone by so fast?' Damn right it has if you weren't around.

I walk away from him, my head shaking like one of those idiot dogs in the back of an idiot's car. Crash into bed at 9 p.m., shattered.

### 11 July 2004

Glorious day off. Julie, John, the Hoults, Karen and daughters, Julian, Fenella and Gabriel minibus back up to Pigg's Peak to visit the mohair-weaving studios at Boshimela.

I spend the day with my family, Emily and Jack, Sindi and Mathokoza, who take us on a short tour of a traditional Swazi village and the Mantenga waterfall. Late lunch with Glenda and John Stephens, joined by the returning Pigg's Peak pilgrims. Great to be able to just sit around and yak with everyone in the late afternoon sun.

## *12 July 2004*

Theatre Club for the *Camelot* audition scene. To save song copyright
costs, I have scripted Nick to sing 'All Things Bright and Beautiful'
in the euphemistically named 'candlelight room', which requires
minimal dressing as it is suitably run down and tatty.

Mutinous noises from the cast and crew as our weekly per diem
has not arrived – this time blame is laid at the door of the Mbabane
Bank, prompting a round of raised eyebrows and muttered 'Oh
yeah?'s.

Olivia Grant, daughter of the director, is playing Ralph's girlfriend, Monica. She is understandably nervous as she has never
filmed anything before and, being a teenager, does not want her dad
making any extra fuss. I feel for her as her first close-up is accompanied by the usual technical camera jargon that we all take for granted,
but with which she is unfamiliar. Very hard as a father *not* to be over-
solicitous in this circumstance, and equally hard for a daughter
feeling she has to prove herself surrounded by such experienced and
talented people. I know she is hugely relieved when her first good
take is done. It's precisely this quality of being shy, wanting to please
and not wanting to make a fuss that makes her perfect to play
Monica, and the reason I risked charges of nepotism.

Miranda shows up at lunchtime, wanting to see her rushes on my
laptop before leaving for London. They have just arrived – nine days
late – and I've not had chance to see them. In the dining-room scene
she instantly spots a microphone cable running down the inside
front of her dress. I ask the sound guy to come and have a look, and
he shrugs his shoulders, puffs some air and walks away. There's no
chance to re-shoot; the only alternative is to cut away in the edit
before we see the cable. To say that Miranda is not best pleased is an
understatement. The antagonism between Charlie and the sound

guys is no secret any more. I am informed by them after lunch that whenever the microphone boom appears during takes, which it increasingly does, I am *not* to say anything!

In the afternoon we shoot the *Camelot* cast list being pinned to the board in the theatre bar, prompting Lady Riva/Celia to explode upon discovering that she is not playing Guinevere, scuppering her plans to impress the incoming royal, and that a Swazi gardener, Dozen/Mathokoza Sibiyu, is playing Lancelot. These fits of pique are innately funny and were typical of the am-dram experience, where someone's age, colour or class were irrelevant as long as they could hit the top notes.

Michael Richards, a South African actor I know from twenty-five years ago, is playing the taciturn, dipsomaniac am-dram play direc-tor Tobias, and has a basso-profundo voice that resonates with the requisite mixture of rage, booze and boredom. In my experience, am-dram actors fell into two camps: the boozers, escapees from domestic tedium and/or stale marriages who resolutely refused to take anything seriously, missed rehearsals, never learnt their lines properly and complained if their social lives were interrupted; and the die-hard fanatics, for whom time stopped still inside the theatre. This made for an unbridgeable gulf, and is an absolute gift for comedy. The disproportionately tunnelled vision and self-aggrandizement required was, come to think of it, *precisely* like directing a film!

### 13 July 2004

Pool-table scene in the bar when Ralph and Vernon, having smoked a joint, and sporting a signature *Clockwork Orange* eyelash, are challenged by a very uptight Charles for taking themselves off to see 'that filth'. The subsequent taunting of Charles is based on the fact that I once inadvertently called an adult friend of our family by his first name, without prefacing it with 'Uncle'. Being fifteen and three-quarters, and having done plays with this chap, I thought it safe to call him by his first name, as I did at the request of most of the other adults by this age. 'Charles' was having none of it and unleashed a tongue-lashing in a high-pitched squeal of rage that I have never forgotten. Julian Wadham plays it dead straight, which makes it all the funnier, whilst Nick and Sid use their pool cues to prod him into apoplexy. It's a delight to recreate this in precisely the place it originally happened, with all its absurd pomp and hilarity.

First kiss between Ralph and Monica, in a dressing room where they fumble and rush to get their costumes on in time for a rehearsal. The room is so cramped it can only accommodate actors and camera crew, so the monitor is outside – meaning that Olivia *doesn't* have to do this in the same room as her dad. She has never kissed a boy before and very sweetly asks if she can play this as if she *hasn't* kissed some-one before. I resolve to make the rehearsal and set-up as technical as possible to get around their understandable anxiety – 'Put this arm here, hold him there, lean in on her right side, mind your camera marks on the floor, don't do it in rehearsal, save it for the take. We will do it from such and such an angle' etc. Blathering really, trying not to make a big deal of it. Nick and Olivia appear very calm and self-possessed.

Glenis Hoult, Nick's mum, my wife and I cram around the play-back monitor and watch dewy eyed as our children kiss each other on film for the first time. It goes really well and they are up for doing it again from different angles. It certainly helps not being in the same room and that they're spared seeing *us* getting emotional about watching them. The two novices deservedly earn their stripes for their first screen kiss, which is totally believable in its simplicity and sincerity.

# SHOOTING

*14 July 2004*

The old axiom that directing a film is like being slowly pecked to death by a flock of pigeons has become that little bit closer to my reality – everyone has questions, and I am adhering to the Ridley Scott dictum: *always* have an answer, even if it means changing your mind five minutes later.

Having dreamt of becoming a professional actor on this selfsame stage thirty years ago, it is truly momentous to return with a film crew, especially as many of the extras either saw or were actually in the original *Camelot* production. Thirty years on and they look as if they are wearing prosthetic old-age make-up.

Very funny shooting the scene with the horse, Who Dares Wins, as it's supposed to be frisky and out of control, but the nag is so docile and old, Fenella has to act as though it's being recalcitrant, and tug and 'control' the reigns by hurling *herself* around.

In order to make the most of our limited time in the theatre, we opt for as many camera angles and set-ups as possible, with the bare minimum of takes, in a frenetic race to cover everything that is scripted. The story-boarding has really come into its own to ensure everything is completed. The carrot keeping us all heads-up is that this is a five-day week with the prospect of an early wrap party tomorrow night – as the majority of the actors will be finished before next weekend.

## 16 July 2004

Last day in the theatre and Mathokoza, with whited-up face and medieval armour, sings his heart out as Lancelot, to a wildly appreciative audience of extras.

The Cinelux Cinema finally closed down three years ago and was bought by Carlos Paiva, with whom I was at junior school, who converted it into a shop selling motorbikes, quads, lawn mowers and all manner of slicing machinery. He has agreed to let us recreate the exterior with the tall neon 'Cinelux' sign he'd saved for me, put up a fake entrance foyer and install a box office. Queues of locals have been forming, convinced that the cinema has reopened.

Clare Marshall, as the Liz Taylor look-alike box-office manageress, is picture-perfect and Nick does his Roger Moore impersonation to charm his way into the screening of *A Clockwork Orange*.

9.30 p.m. wrap and there's a mad scramble to clear everything up before heading for the wrap party at the open-air House on Fire Theatre in Malkerns. This is an extraordinary venue created by Jiggs Thorn, whose late mother Jenny was a great friend and one of the original barefoot hippies who blew into Swaziland in 1969, and who subsequently set up Gone Rural, a collective of Swazi women weavers whose work is now exported and sold in Liberty's and the like. She was fiercely independent, determined to live as a white African rather than a colonial expat, a passionate and life-enhancing spirit, whose life was prematurely ended by leukaemia two years ago.

Jiggs has employed Swazi sculptors to help create this unique theatre, used mainly for visiting musicians and singers, and it's the most idiosyncratic and perfect place for our farewell party. I knew that I would not be much good at making a big speech without blubbing, so I went round to everyone who had given so much of themselves to this film and thanked them individually instead.

# SHOOTING

All the Swazilanders involved voiced regret at our pending departure in ten days, saying they had never experienced anything quite like our 'invasion' before. Emily Watson paid me the sweetest goodnight compliment, saying, 'I'm sure you will direct many movies in the future.' At this moment, I want to believe her and am profoundly grateful for her faith.

## 17 July 2004

Little more than a week left to complete shooting, and we are still on schedule. *Just!* I realize that in spite of my inexperience as a director, knowing what I want has been an enormous advantage. Almost without exception, whenever I have wavered or been persuaded to do something against my instincts, the result has been woolly and indecisive.

My wife Joan's respect for me as a director has been a great gift, and something I have always felt I wanted to prove to her as well as myself. Earning respect for something 'new' after twenty-one years together has real significance, especially as I admire *her* work so much.

## 18 July 2004

5 a.m. call – too dark to run. Filming at Malkerns Cricket Club had to be rescheduled from Saturday to Sunday as the citrus fruit and pineapple canning factory next door is working six days a week to cope with the harvest, and the noise would drown out all dialogue. Zoe Dean-Smith has recruited a cricket team of Swazilanders to play in the background, whilst Lady Riva grills Ruby and Gwen in the tea stand.

All the cricketers pitch up wearing Nike trainers as opposed to old-fashioned white spiked boots, so we fix masking tape over the logos and ask second unit cameraman Justin Fouche to frame up above them. Justin is on hand to shoot as much cricket footage as possible, including slow-motion bowling and close-ups on balls hitting stumps. This footage is required for the time-lapse sequence in which, as an alternative to computer-generated imagery, the younger Ralph (Zac) morphs into the older Ralph (Nick). Each actor is also filmed against the scoreboard with the numbers 69, 70 and 71 flapping over to indicate the passing years.

The five-day week has had an obvious impact on everyone, with a huge upsurge in energy and refreshed faces all round. Plus perfect weather.

The only real wobble is the bum direction I gave Celia, encouraging her to be too arch and theatrical in Lady Riva's verbal dismissal of Ruby. Emily comes up and quietly suggests we ground everything in reality, which is the perfect thing to say and I am grateful for her tact and diplomacy. Celia feels much better and plays the scene more effectively. It is a real measure of the generosity and care of both Emily and Celia that they took the trouble to 're-direct' me so diplomatically, without making me feel like a total toss-box!

I have often wondered whether the crew on any film, whilst setting up all their technical gear, get frustrated by actors and directors tying themselves up in knots, trying to make a scene work, before the camera rolls. My feelings are that even if the rehearsal seems indulgent or excessively time-consuming, it is always worth every second. Once it feels right, the actual shooting gets done relatively quickly. I think it's fatal to start shooting a scene when everyone is not on the same page in the hope that it will somehow work itself out, rather like fooling yourself that if the script is not watertight to begin with some acting or filming magic will transform it. In my experience it never does – if it's not on the page, it won't be on the screen.

Carlos Paiva turned up with his family for lunch. I last saw Carlos when he was twelve, an insouciant scally with an anarchic streak and a mass of black curly hair. During lunch I tried to reconcile that boy with the successful middle-aged balding businessman in front of me, who prides himself on being a very strict father! When I told his teenage son and daughter what their dad was like at school in 1969, I could see they thought I was talking cobblers.

Olivia and Celia both end the day feeling very off colour. A quick trip to see Dr Stephens, who conveniently lives a mile away from our hotel, confirms that they have been bitten by ticks. Olivia bursts into tears, convinced she will have to go back to London like Alex Oakley and miss the end of the filming. The good doctor prescribes antibiotics and reassures them that they will be better within a couple of days.

Having given Karen Jones, our script-supervisor supremo, a lift to and from locations throughout the shoot, I have had the privilege of being able to go through the day's events with her properly. I've had the most supportive and professional advice from her I could wish for as a first-timer, and I am hugely indebted to her. She has looked out for me ceaselessly, made sure I've eaten when I've forgotten to, made me laugh when I've needed to and provided me with the wealth of her experience in a way that I have no way of adequately measuring. We have worked seamlessly as a team and I hope we can do this again 'the next time'. Whilst being incredibly kind-hearted, she is also a real stickler for detail and has made sure everything in the script is adhered to, which as the writer is something I am *really* grateful for. All this, and her ability to 'correct' an actor's lines between takes in a way that is never admonishing or intrusive, makes her a real gem.

### 19 July 2004

Late start at 1 p.m. as we are shooting till midnight.

Since the demise of the Cinelux and drive-in cinemas, the convention centre at the Royal Swazi Hotel is the only venue in the country that can show films, and it's where we shoot the interior of the Cinelux for the *Clockwork Orange* sequence.

Having been so determined to get in to see the film, nothing prepared me for the shock of Malcolm McDowell's all-seeing stare in the opening sequence. It was also a moment of rebellion and I felt that if I stared back hard enough, I would somehow be empowered to face down anything that came my way.

Julian and Fenella, playing Charles and June, are spied snogging by Nick and Sid a couple of rows behind. The boys are scripted to react as though a cat has just shat itself in front of them. Their actual reaction was to laugh, because Julian enthusiastically snogged Fenella for real and seemed to have gone deaf to the word 'cut'. There was much teasing and ribbing, as he didn't actually have to snog her so passionately, especially when the camera wasn't rolling. He gamely replied that he had been divorced for a couple of years, and Fenella being so gorgeous, why waste the opportunity?

I tried to describe to Nick and Sid the frisson of seeing this controversial film as a teenager in the early seventies, but the advent of video, DVD, cable, satellite and the Internet has now pretty much cancelled out the shock value films can have, and I felt like an old fogey trying to convey the risk and thrill of it. They humoured me with some concentrated nodding, but couldn't entirely disguise the glaze in their eyes.

This reminded me of when I walked in on my then twelve-year-old daughter watching the DVD of *Sliding Doors* at the moment when Jean Tripplehorn is sitting on top of John Hannah, shagging.

I instantly panicked, assuming she had accessed some soft-porn channel, only to be told with total nonchalance that she had watched the film about six times already. I used to wonder at what moment I would know that I was older, and this was certainly one of them.

While we shoot in the convention centre, an old period banger is driven into the vast foyer, parked in a blackout tent and lit for the scene in which a car full of teenagers drives from the Theatre Club down to the 'cuddle puddle' in the Ezulweni Valley. Originally a hot muddy pond at the bottom of the MacDonalds' farm, it has since been chi-chi'd up into a proper mineral water swimming pool and health spa.

Gary filled up the back windows with balloons to disguise the fact that the car was stationary, and crammed in six teenagers: Nick, Sid, Olivia, Will Williamson, Gary's son who had just arrived, and Karen's daughters Jess and Robyn, all chanting, 'Cu-ddle pu-ddle, cu-ddle pu-ddle.'

Saturday-night entertainment for Mbabane teenagers in the seventies was found at the Red Feather disco in the Swazi Inn Hotel, a beautiful thatched colonial bungalow which was later burned down in an insurance scam, but which was then replete with Tudor-beamed bar and dartboard, where we whiled away the time till the disco started at 10.30. The 'disco' was a small dance floor in the corner of the dining room with a single glitter ball. The speciality on the menu was monkey-gland steak – not actually anything to do with its name, but a dish we enjoyed persuading visitors to the country to try, especially at Sunday lunch when you could see monkeys leaping around in the surrounding trees.

It was important to know a teenager old enough to drive, as the hotel was halfway down the treacherous Malegwane Hill, and not walkable. The ritual of getting drunk or stoned, dancing and finding someone to snog by 12.30, if you weren't already attached, was strictly adhered to. You knew you were either made up or done for by the time the single ultraviolet light was switched on to accompany Bread singing 'Baby I'm-A Want You' or 'Guitar Man' signalling closing time. After which, everyone crammed into and onto anything with wheels and careered off down to the cuddle puddle. It was always crowded with late-night revellers, wearing either undies or nothing, for some bacchanalia and de-flowerings.

Lynne-Anne negotiated with the German owner of the health spa to allow us to shoot there tonight, requiring a massive effort from the lighting crew, who installed underwater lamps and coloured bulbs strung across the steaming water, illuminating the surrounding huts, trees and bamboo. Sheena provided everyone with seventies bikinis and shorts. Gary installed a ramp from the side of the pool onto the little concrete island for Julie Walters to cross for her character's impromptu post-*Camelot* striptease. We cajoled as many of the cast as possible to brave the freezing night air and spend four hours in the hot water.

First up is the second screen kiss between Nick and Olivia. No direction is required other than 'Please move *your* head to the left a little more, and *yours* to the right.' Julie acts patently sozzled and rallies the crowd with a doggerel version of 'Rule, Britannia' which everyone joins in with, climbing onto the island to conga with her, then all jumping back into the water. The last gasp of Empire, before the formalities of Independence Day that follow. As usual, Julie requires minimum rehearsal and goes for her song and striptease at full throttle to enormous cheers. We complete shooting well before midnight.

The beauty of filming here is that most of the locations are about fifteen minutes away from each other. It's the drive to and from sets that normally end up making the days so long and exhausting. In this instance the hotel is five minutes away, and with another late call tomorrow everyone's spirits are very high, none more so than Nick Hoult and his mum, Glenis, as his sisters Roz and Clarista arrived the day before. They have been apart for months as Nick came out to

Swaziland pretty much straight after shooting *The Weather Man* in Chicago.

Glenis and Emily Watson have organized a collection of children's clothes for a Swazi orphanage and have plans to get donations from England flown out via British Airways, as Glenis's husband is a BA pilot. Karen Jones, Gabriel and Emily have already contributed food, school stationery and toys and included a memo on the daily call sheet asking cast and crew to hand in whatever they can contribute to the production office. Given the devastating reality that an estimated forty per cent of the Swazi population are HIV-positive, thousands of children are left parentless.

*20 July 2004*

The main unit is called for 11 a.m. to prep for the Independence scene at Somhlolo Stadium, where the original ceremony took place, but the second unit is up at 6 a.m. Charlie Watson has scouted out a nearby location with the vertiginous Lobamba Mountains as a backdrop for the multiple car and motorbike drive-bys to be shot with doubles of Gabriel, Nick and Sid. We do, however, have Zac, which is a bonus, who is able to work so early as he is not in the scenes after lunch.

It's very cold, but we are blessed with a clear sky and residual early morning mist. Charlie seems far happier dealing with machines than humans. 'You will thank me for all this footage in the edit, I assure you,' he says, and I know he's dead right.

At the stadium, Jen Sale has procured 147 extras, which Sheena and her team have dressed in everything from traditional Swazi Mahiyas, or warrior regalia, to Western floral two-pieces and cream suits and pith helmets worn by the outgoing Brits. The trick will be to make this number of extras appear to be much larger, and instead of everyone filling the length of three rows of seats, it's better to stagger them over a dozen rows in a triangular 'wedge', so that through the viewfinder it looks as if there are crowds just out of sight. All the old cine cameras and binoculars I collected at Portobello market over the past couple of years come into their own today.

I intend cross-cutting between the crowd filmed today and the wonderful Super 8 footage of the original ceremony kindly lent me by Jan and Alistair Smart, who left Swaziland after Independence. The distinctive sound these cameras make will be added in post-production. As the whole story is told from Nick/Ralph's point of view, it is plausible that we the audience 'see' Independence through his eyes, and his Super 8 footage.

The warriors, bare-breasted women and crowd of Swazi extras need little encouragement to erupt and ululate when told that their King is arriving to receive the scroll and emblem of Independence from the British. Sheena and Chrissie have dressed and wigged an extra to play Princess Margaret. John Carlisle is rigged out in full uniformed splendour, groaning with medals and topped off with a white-feather-plumed hat.

Having anticipated that shooting would be very lengthy and arduous, it turns out to be relatively simple due to everyone being in the stadium stands, either seated or standing up, when the royals 'arrive'. It's emotionally charged on many levels as it's also the last day for Julian, Julie, Caroline, Olivia, Celia, Sindi, Clare Marshall, Michael Richards and many of the local extras who have featured in so many scenes.

A film 'family' is in many ways ideal in that you are free to choose who you want to socialize with, without any actual familial obligation. Being on location and working long hours playing intensely emotional scenes facilitates very close friendships that in other circumstances would take years to develop. The downside is that very often what seemed like the basis for lifelong friendship is illusory – meeting up again after a couple of years, you discover that the film experience is all you really have in common.

# SHOOTING

Pierre has prepped the crew to shoot until 11 p.m., but by 5 p.m.
I have everything I need and call our earliest wrap yet, just as the sun
disappears. The day is perfectly topped off with a concert given by
Mathokoza and his choir in the convention centre. Being the obser-
vant humorist that he is, he makes a speech that satirizes all our
technical jargon, conducts his choir to sing a variety of traditional
Swazi songs and then calls me onto the stage to hand over his gift of
a traditional Swazi stick, claiming that 'no Swazi should ever travel
through life without a weapon and good-luck talisman'.

I attempted to respond coherently but got somewhat choked up
along the way, jumped off the stage with my stick aloft and eyes-a-
full.

## 21 July 2004

End-of-term feeling, end-of-term humour. Suddenly intimate doing
a scene with only two actors and a Mercedes in Murray Street,
renamed Umpohlo Street, back up in Mbabane. Nick/Ralph is
aimlessly wandering around the day after the gun episode with his
father, filmed weeks ago.

Emily/Ruby is at the wheel, tracking him down to persuade
him to come home. We choose a tall avenue of pine trees to make
fourteen-year-old, six-foot-three Nick appear smaller. Well, that's
the idea.

Like Miranda, Emily is an expert driver and handles the old stick
shift with aplomb, reversing and stopping at her precise camera
marks each time. Doubtless this sounds like a doddle, but all the
technical requirements have to be dealt with and the scene has to be
played while making it look as effortless as possible.

The scene focuses on Nick as he ponders why his father hits the
booze every time his ex-wife appears, triggering Ruby to decide to
withdraw from the marriage. The meat of the scene is shot whilst

the car is stationary to avoid the distraction of engine noise or using a tracking shot. This involves mega-close-ups, and as it is largely unspoken, Emily mines every possible nuance to express Ruby's turmoil and demands more takes than she ever has done before, pushing and testing for every possibility.

If I hadn't fully recognized it before, her work today leaves me in no doubt why directors rush to work with her and why she is so particular in her choice of roles. She has an emotional bravery and a willingness to go all the way, and is astonishingly unostentatious and determined.

The second scene of the day is set outside Sid/Vernon's bedroom, both he and Ralph having been grounded for sneaking in to see *A Clockwork Orange*. Vernon compounds their offence by offering Ralph a hit of his joint. It's Sid's final day and he is given a vigorous round of applause by everyone after his last take.

Julie and Maisie, Julian and Fenella, Celia and Angus and John Carlisle have all stopped by for their farewell location lunch en route to Jo'burg and London. More applause and tears all round. It's not as if we have all been together out here for that long – it's the sheer intensity of it all and the personal investment people have made in the story.

Spend the remainder of the day shooting in my old St Mark's Primary School classroom, which has the same blackboard, graffiti and compass-gouged desks thirty-five years later. We numbered twenty-two to a classroom in 1969; now there are fifty crammed into the same space.

Zac Fox has been kitted out in the uniform, and has learnt enough Siswati to make rudimentary conversation with his classmates, all of whom are extras for the afternoon. Tony Hatton, my old history master, is on hand to play Mr Parker, and asks me how I want him to play the scene. 'Just like you did when you were my teacher,' I say. Which he does impeccably.

# SHOOTING

## *22 July 2004*

Mbuluzi Mission School in Pine Valley, a few miles east of Mbabane. Unlike St Mark's, this school is in pristine condition with long colonnaded verandas, and is the location for an outdoor classroom inspection by Gabriel/Harry on the day his wife left him. Sibusiso Mamba plays a Catholic priest-cum-teacher.

This is a replay of the day my mother woke me at dawn, when I was ten, to tell me she was leaving, wouldn't be coming back, and that instead of school today I could go on a schools-inspection trip with my father.

It feels simultaneously like it happened yesterday and in another life. My parents' divorce forced a 'double' view of people and events in my mind – what appeared on the surface, and what I knew was going on underneath – which led to a lifelong curiosity as to what makes people the way they are. A blueprint for being an actor/ writer/director if ever there was one.

My father's schizoid alcoholism was characterized by his charming and generous persona by day in acute contrast to the morose and destructive demon he became at night when drunk. Consequently every friend we had existed as two versions of themselves inside my head – the friends who filled our house with whom he was witty, flirtatious and provocative, but who, when he was whiskey'd up, would be verbally annihilated once they'd left. His character assassinations made me feel guilty and two-faced, inculcating a lifelong sense of being at once an outsider and an insider.

I'm not singing the Billie Holiday blues here, simply trying to make sense of how I am able to revisit my past, via this film, without having a nervous breakdown in the process. I am repeatedly asked out here how I can bear to recreate something so personal in public, and to me it seems the most creative way of making sense of these events. The more personal and truthful you dare to be, the greater the likelihood that other people might recognize their own experiences. Well, that's the theory, anyway; the proof will be whether people pay to see the film or not.

Sid Mitchell drops by for his farewell lunch, exchanges phone numbers with everyone and is given a huge send-off. A.D. Van Wyk, the car supremo, has invited cast and crew to a spit-roast-lamb supper at his Quatermain's pub near Mantenga. With a day off tomorrow, it's like an end-of-term knees-up – food, dancing and four laptops lined up along the bar featuring slide shows of all the on-set photos taken by the crew.

### 23 July 2004

Mozambique for our day off. I drove with Emily, Jack, Joan and Olivia. I hadn't been since the overnight revolution and mass Portuguese evacuation in the mid-seventies, when the capital was called Lourenço Marques, since renamed Maputo.

The moment we crossed the border and queued up in the Mozambique customs hall, the contrast between the two countries was painfully apparent. It looked like a refugee encampment. The aggressive officials took half an hour to process our passports, which were put through more cross-checks than at Checkpoint Charlie. The roads were potholed to hell, and the barren countryside was devoid of any agriculture, with many burned-out buildings. Maputo looked like Beirut with palm trees. Everything was on its last legs, pockmarked with shrapnel and numerous burned-out vehicles. Felt conspicuously white, wealthy and unwelcome. What did I expect after a thirty-year civil war that has decimated the economy and land-mined so many limbs?

Drove on feeling guilty at every turn for thinking I could come here for a relaxing day off. The road signs were in Portuguese and whenever we stopped to ask for directions, no one spoke English. Finally we made it to the Costa Del Sol beachfront restaurant, an art-deco establishment that was the number-one port of call in its heyday, and were totally surrounded by beggars and curio sellers. After eating duff prawns with mouthfuls of guilt and regret for ever coming here, we walked along the flat, muddy beach, then decided to head back. Having taken a wrong turning, we were sirened to stop by a pair of traffic police from the *Midnight Express* casting dept. I was ordered to get out of the car and walk away with them. Convinced I was going to be fleeced of all my money and my passport, I was rescued, at this sphincter-winking moment, by a Portuguese businessman in a fancy motor who mercifully pulled up beside me, barked commands at the policemen and suggested in broken English that I follow him and he would guide us out of the city. I don't know who he was or why they listened to him, but the sight of familiar faces in my car as I walked back to it was something for which I felt profoundly grateful. I had a dose of the shakes for a good half-hour and accelerated out of Maputo and Mozambique as fast as I could.

Swazilanders had warned that there were roadblocks to fleece tourists and scams at every turn, but my curiosity overrode these warnings. This only increased my guilt and shame. The relief as we drove back into Swaziland was smile-wide.

### *24 July 2004*

Penultimate day of filming, twenty-five degrees, beautiful, clear and sunny. We head for Phuzamoya train station in the south of Swaziland. Very early exodus from the first-world luxuries of the Royal Swazi Hotel down through the sparsely populated countryside dotted with mud huts, cattle enclosures, patches of corn and a sense of time suspended.

Gary has dressed the industrial railway siding to resemble the most basic passenger station possible. The old steam train, exactly like the one on which I went to and from boarding school, has been hired and railed in from South Africa, where it is used for tourist trips. The setting is a perfect John Ford / Edward Hopper landscape – lonely, dusty and isolated with tracks stretching in both directions into the far distance.

There are forty-five extras to get on and off the train. The camera department are very excited by the prospect of filming the train from every possible angle. Justin Fouche is back to do second-unit train coverage. As we cannot turn the train around, it has to be shunted backwards and forwards with the engine 'cheated' out of shot when reversing, to disguise its absence. The steam and screech of brakes and whistle are all in full and wondrous working order. We begin with Zac's departure and end with the return of Nick as the older Ralph. The aged, fanatical mechanics proudly steam and shunt the grand old boiler back and forth till we have everything covered.

As we prepare to shoot the scene of a drunk Harry fetching older Ralph from the station, long after the other passengers have left, we are fast running out of daylight. Despite grumblings from Gabe and Nick, they complete the scene with minimal rehearsal time and the maximum number of camera set-ups, but both are worried that they have been so rushed that we don't have the scene in the can. I try my best to reassure them that I wouldn't wrap unless we had it.

The 'will he, won't he show up' syndrome of waiting to be picked up by a drunk father is something I am really grateful not to have to deal with ever again. There is an awful conundrum in wanting to see him so badly, yet dreading how long the wait will be. The longer the wait, the more hatefully drunk and out of control he would be. His arrival would be accompanied by the habitually slurred rhetoric of 'Have I ever let you down?' My emphatic 'Yes!' fell on deaf ears.

There's nothing like getting to the last couple of days to flush out MC and co., busily trying to look busy, which prompts raised eyebrows and exchanged smiles amongst the rest of us. I doubt anything is going to change how the cast and crew view them at this late stage.

Gabriel and Emily have especially early calls tomorrow morning and are understandably aggrieved that they are not able to stay in the Mkaya Game Reserve, which is where we are spending the night, due to the limited number of beds available. MC and co. are staying in their place. Despite the much-lamented exclusion of Gabriel and Emily, there is a magical atmosphere at our final communal meal in the Mkaya campsite, lit by oil lamps, eating around a huge open fire, the stars in the night sky and wild-animal sounds everywhere.

### 25 July 2004

Emily and Gabriel are picked up at 5 a.m. to travel south to the game reserve. The crew in the campsite are up at 6.30 a.m. and convoyed to the quarry in the middle of the reserve, a location chosen for its 360-degree view of the Bushveld, from where Harry reflects about his life as a white man in Africa. He challenges Dr Mzimba with his conclusion, 'Your tribe wouldn't give a damn if we all dropped dead from tick-bite fever tomorrow,' to which the doctor retorts, 'You're dead right.'

Towards the end, my father was convinced he had wasted his life endeavouring to improve education standards, convinced that the Swazis in particular and Africa in general would be best served by the wholesale exodus of all Europeans. I wish he could have seen the massive Swazi turnout at his funeral.

A cock-up in communications leads to the two-hour delay in the camera and sound crews arriving from the unit base in Phuzamoya. By the time we turn over, the weather has clouded over so much that it rather spoils the point of being up here in the first place.

I had expected Gabriel to be in pyjamas and wrapped in a blanket for Harry's last look at Africa, but he is kitted out in safari suit with a rifle on his lap, looking like the colonial white hunter from every other movie ever set in Africa. It's too late to get his clothes changed. This is the only time during the whole shoot that I have had to film a scene that I know in my guts is not quite right.

We move our reduced unit convoy to another part of the reserve for our final location lunch beside a small lake. Rangers advise us to keep our distance from the rhino and her calf drinking on the far side of the water, flanked by a pair of giraffes. The familiar sounds and smells of the Bushveld are overwhelmingly nostalgic. In 1964, my father was given a Carnegie grant to do a six-month lecture tour on African education in the United States, during which time I lived with my aunt and uncle on their cattle-and-cotton ranch in the south of Swaziland. The thorn trees, scrub vegetation, red soil and caws of the birds are all exactly as I remember them.

After completing the close-up footage on the back of the Land Rover, when Harry attempts to shoot an elephant, we get word from Ted Riley's team of trackers that there is an actual herd near by. Immediately, the Steadicam is strapped onto a jeep which follows behind Mathokoza, John, Nicholas, Emily and Gabriel. Daylight and film stock are both running out fast. On the way to the herd, we pass more rhino and film Gabriel pointing at them in that unique golden-hour light of an early African evening.

Emily is concerned about being close to the elephants, but boldly agrees to let us try to film actors and animals in the same shot. It's getting noticeably darker by the minute as we dust along the dirt track. Suddenly there they are, all grazing together. We slow to a crawl and the rangers speak to the animals in low, reassuring tones. I tap the camera operator's shoulder to shift focus from the elephants onto the actors, then back again. The film stock in the camera finally runs out, ending our shoot, in the middle of the bush, at dusk, on schedule and on budget.

As we obviously can't yell out loud, we all grin and punch the air in triumph.

Once we are far enough away from the magnificent herd, everyone breaks out cheering and clapping. The synchronicity of film stock running out when it did and the conjunction of actors and animals in the last glimmer of dusk is momentarily beguiling enough to make me believe there is a god. Chrissie Baker says, 'You see, Richard, you *do* have a guardian angel looking after you.' At this moment, in the sheer euphoria and relief that we have actually completed, I am willing to believe anything.

Back at the lake, Charlie announces, 'That's a wrap,' for the final time. Everyone drives back to the hotel for a late farewell dinner. I feel triumphant – even if the film never gets released or seen by anyone, nothing can ever take away the forty-carat gleaming pleasure we have had in each other's company over these past couple of months. I've worked on thirty-one feature films and never experienced anything that comes close to this.

Gabriel is at pains to point out to the younger actors that this has been a unique and life-changing experience. 'Don't know why, don't know how, but believe me, it's been *spiritual*.' Nobody disagrees.

Later on that night I stand on the hotel balcony in the cold moonlight, naked as the night I was born, for the birth and delivery of my movie, forty-seven years and two months since popping out of my mother!

### 26 July 2004

Took the morning assembly at my old school, Waterford-Kamhlaba, fielding questions and trying to bridge the years between myself as a gawky, painfully skinny, spotty teenager and the middle-aged family man I now am. This was on the same stage I did plays with Mandela's daughters, when their father's release seemed impossible in our lifetime.

Race down to Johnny and Stella Masson's to return the biscuit tins, ceremonial sword, pith helmet and OBE medal they kindly lent me, then back to the hotel to pack. Martin Jaubert, MC's sidekick, knocks on my door and demands all the DVD rushes to give to the South African co-producers 'who have not seen any of them yet'. I tell him that as *I* have yet to receive all the rushes from Paris and have had to wait so long for them, they can easily wait a couple of days for their copies to be sent from France.

Lunch with Emily and Gabriel at which they pledge to do whatever they can to promote the film when it's finally edited and ready for release.

Drive to Jo'burg and meet the cast and crew in the airport. Homeward bound, and the relief is bone deep.

### 27 July 2004

On reflection it has been the most intense and staggeringly stretching thing I have ever done and I feel stupendous. I love my new job. Back home and I'm happy as a humming bird. An email from Gabriel's agent Teri Hayden in Dublin says that Gabriel told her it had been the most amazingly positive experience of his career.

Gary, Chrissie and Will, who are still in Swaziland on safari, call to say that the heavens had opened and it has been raining solidly since we left.

### 28 July 2004

Despite being told that the outstanding two and a half weeks of unseen rushes would be sent, *nothing* has arrived from Paris.

On the flight back from Swaz, I'd read a review of *Camelot* which has serendipitously opened at Regent's Park Open Air Theatre. This is too good an opportunity to miss for a *Wah-Wah* reunion. Ring around and rally the troops.

# POST-PRODUCTION

3.30 p.m. meeting at my agent's office, with lawyers, Emily Watson and Scion lawyer and co-producer Julia Blackman. The agenda is to try and get an overview of what lies ahead in post-production.

I had put in a courtesy call to Zygy Komasi at Redbus, the distributors, to ask if he wanted to attend, only to be told they had not heard a word from MC in over two months. Apparently she is focused on 'artistic control and final cut'. It is in my contract that as long as I produce a director's cut that is 105 minutes or less, I have creative control.

*Camelot* cast reunion – Sid, Celia and Angus, Fenella, Olivia, Emily and Jack, Joan and I, Nick, Glenis, Roz and Clarista Hoult meet for a pre-show picnic in Regent's Park. Julie Walters can't make it as she is at an agricultural sheep show in Sussex, Julian Wadham is on the Isle of Wight with his sons, Gabriel is in Cape Town and Miranda Richardson is filming *Harry Potter*.

As we file out of the theatre afterwards, we whisper to one another in hallowed am-dram tradition, 'Our production was *much* better!'

Email from Jane at Boshimela: 'After you all left, there was only a telephone pole left in the field where the unit base and catering marquee had been set up, and the staff were utterly perplexed and asked if the whole *Wah-Wah* event had in fact been a dream.'

## 1–10 August 2004

Went to Nice for a holiday before starting the edit. Isabelle Dedieu is working on the first assembly. Could not sleep properly, still waiting for the remaining rushes to arrive and suffering *Wah-Wah* withdrawal. Nothing quite prepared me for the sense of anti-climax as I fried inertly on the beach after months of such frenetic activity. The only question I was asked came from a waiter, enquiring what I wanted for lunch.

## 11 August 2004

6.10 p.m. flight to Paris, booked by Loma Nasha. Not really surprised to discover that they have failed to provide a proper reference number or electronic ticket verification. Phone calls back and forth are made, I miss take-off and finally catch a later plane once the office has sorted the ticket out.

Writer-directors Harry Hook and Peter Capaldi have both warned me that seeing the first edited assembly is an inevitably depressing let-down. I brace myself during the fifteen-minute walk to the edit room in rue du Cherche-Midi, and meet Isabelle and her assistant Liza. The room has a two-seater Ikea sofa, a couple of swivel chairs, TV, Avid editing screens on a long desk, and a wall covered in post-cards with scene numbers and headings in chronological order from 1 to 142. An opaque sliding-glass door and entry keypad separates us from the other edit suites up and down the corridor.

All of us are somewhat formal and apprehensive. I am left alone to watch their first 'version' of the film. Almost from the first frame, I started scribbling notes and ideas. Without any music to connect and bridge scenes, or any writer/director input, it all feels very level and measured, one scene lolloping after the other. I wasn't bored, but nor was I moved – more bemused than anything, itching to get my hands on it and start trying things out and chopping away. Essentially felt like it didn't have a point of view, and I was surprised, seeing it all strung together, how obvious it was which scenes needed to be cut out completely and where to snip and speed it all up. Writing the screenplay was one version, the actual shooting another, and the third will come through the edit.

Isabelle times her return to the minute and is clearly anxious for my response. I feel guilty that I am unable to thrill and froth and can only be circumspectly complimentary. Her vast experience ameliorates my reticence and after lunch we begin at the beginning. Her policy is to start cutting and re-cutting scenes at speed, without reviewing the new cuts we have made along the way, feeling that to do so prevents a rhythm developing.

Bruno Daniault, the Loma Nasha post-production manager, comes in to explain why Liza has not had delivery of a second Avid computer yet, to do her work on. The exchanged glances between Isabelle and Liza make me wonder if they have heard this all before.

I sit beside Isabelle and she starts re-editing according to my notes. As she has done her first version, I am granted the courtesy of doing mine. The speed and skill with which she handles the computer is amazing. The relief that we are able to work in such immediate harmony cannot be overestimated, and confirms our instincts that we would make a good team after only a single meeting that lasted thirty minutes, three months ago.

We work non-stop from 2 p.m. till 8.30 p.m. and reduce the first ten minutes of the film down to eight. Liza works out that we could reduce the first 120 assembled minutes to 100 in a couple of weeks. They express their relief that I am not precious about cutting ruthlessly and willing to try things out. So far so good.

Isabelle says she has had many difficulties because of the problem of actors' eye-lines crossing in the wrong direction, which Karen Jones was always so worried about. This has forced her to cut scenes in a way that weren't her first choice. Director of photography and camera operator are patently different jobs and skills for me, and I resolve to work with two people in the future if given another chance to direct.

### 12 August 2004

Start at 9.30 a.m., short lunch break, then work through till 9 p.m. Feels like another full circle completed: begin a film alone with your laptop writing, get your cast and crew, cart off on location, shoot with an army of people and return to a desk, staring at images, alone in a dark room save for the editor.

The thrill of being able to reshape a scene is a real surprise. There is a constant challenge to find 'short cuts' whilst retaining the most information or drama or emotion possible. Every scene has to justify its presence and move the narrative on – if it fails, the scissors come out, no matter how beautifully acted or filmed it might be.

Isabelle pays me the compliment of telling me I have good editorial instincts, which cannot be learned – after weeks of me bolstering and reassuring the cast and crew, her appraisal is especially welcome.

Isabelle, who originally trained as a dancer but grew too tall, is calm, compassionate and has infinite patience and innate kindness. Liza is librarian quiet, fastidious and frustrated that she is unable to do any work until we are finished, as Bruno has yet to provide her with her own computer. This has been ongoing for a while, apparently.

Within no time at all, the three of us find ourselves on the most intimate terms and no subject is taboo. Opinions about every take of every scene are bounced back and forth.

### 13 August 2004

It is extraordinary to spend all day discussing how best to edit scenes with two people who had nothing to do with the actual shooting, and are solely guided by the rushes and the story. It requires a conscious effort on my part not to let the on-set activities influence my judgement, but the advantage of the editor being separated from the shoot is clear.

Bruno says that the sound editor will be French and all the work done in Paris, which seems to me to be *contrary* to the DCMS co-production stipulations. I call Scion, and Julia Blackman assures me that she will clarify this. The concentration required for editing is all-encompassing, and having to deal with other issues after a day's work is exhausting. Isabelle suggests I contact Dean Humphreys, a highly experienced English sound editor who regularly works with Roman Polanski and has done a hundred and thirty films, so I check his availability and post him the script.

Fly back to Nice for the weekend to join my family who are on holiday there till the end of August.

### 18 August 2004

Bruno was 'mistaken': Dean Humphreys is appointed sound editor!

The turnover of staff in MC's office continues apace, and a new assistant called Laetitia asks that I provide all the Warner Brothers *Clockwork Orange* paperwork, despite giving it to them four months ago.

### 19 August 2004

Cut another four minutes and all going great guns. Isabelle likens the process to cooking – reducing and reducing the sauce in order to concentrate the flavours and make them as strong as possible.

Like in gardening, pruning scenes makes them stronger. Very energizing process.

### 21 August 2004

Dinner in Nice with Gabriel Byrne, en route from Africa to New York, who in true peripatetic fashion pitched up unexpectedly and picked up our conversation as though he'd just popped round the corner for a minute. Odd feeling hearing about actors' next jobs, knowing that I will be consumed by this film for the next nine months of post-production.

Dean Humphreys calls to say the script made him laugh out loud and cry. Clearly the man for this job!

### 23 August 2004

We have nicknamed Bruno 'the flea', as he is annoying and difficult to pin down. He has still failed to deliver the Avid machine for Liza to work on – in frustration we phone the Avid hire company to find out what the delay is all about, to discover that the booking wasn't confirmed and the machine has been hired out elsewhere.

In the same way that time is suspended when writing, we lose all sense of it whilst editing, and though the hours are long, it is very stimulating and challenging.

## POST-PRODUCTION

Cutting the Independence and funeral footage takes much longer as there are so many choices and options. Felt overwhelmed, but moved forward as soon as we stuck to the dictum that everything has to be from Ralph's point of view. As in the writing and shooting, it proves to be an inviolate compass. My confidence has a terrible way of yo-yoing, but Isabelle is very calming and reassuring. The wobbles come when we have spent hours cutting individual scenes into a sequence, only to find that when all run together, something doesn't quite work or fit. I have an ongoing worry that there isn't enough 'story' to hold it all together. Will it hold an audience's attention? Isabelle says that this is one of the most common bleats from writers and directors, and not to let it stymie the work.

Isabelle, like Gabriel, had worried that I might be so emotionally involved with my story that I wouldn't be capable of sufficient detachment and objectivity – and she continues to be pleased that I am all too willing to cut a swathe through the material. The writing process cured any preciousness about making cuts. Simply part of the process.

### 24 August 2004

Completed my first edit from Isabelle's first 120-minute version at 8 p.m. It runs at just over 105 minutes, which means we have excised fifteen minutes in ten days. *Thrilled!*

### 25 August 2004

I was very excited and nervous about watching the new version, but depressed, disheartened and disillusioned once I'd done so. Despite

Isabelle's and Liza's reassurances to the contrary, felt like I'd blobbed spectacularly, and wanted to run away. My *usual* calm and collected response . . . !

Grumped through lunch and started from the very beginning working from the notes I had scribbled down throughout the gruesome morning's screening. Despite reinstating some scenes, we managed to cut a further two minutes by the end of the day by trimming elsewhere.

My wife, who has seen so many films mid-edit in order to make dialect or accent notes for directors and actors, confirmed Isabelle's diagnosis that without music and sound effects, every film seems deadly. Just hope they are right. Feel as if my skin has been torn off and I just want to hide away. Must sleep on it!

### 27 August 2004

The funeral scene has been cut in half, excising the priest jumping into the grave and attempting to raise Harry from the dead. Even though it actually happened, I can see the argument for cutting it out as it breaks the emotional line of the story, with its Monty Python-meets-Joe Orton insanity, and at this point in the story, you need to be moved by Harry's demise, not jolted into uneasy laughter.

Likewise the safari scenes in the game reserve. In the context of the whole, they feel tagged on – having had no scenes of wild animals in the rest of the film, it looks as if we are giving the audience a last-minute dose of traditional safari footage that is the cliché of every white-folk-in-Africa film ever made.

The flea finally pitches up with an Avid for Liza.

Make a video copy of the latest cut to take away for the weekend and test-screen for my wife and daughter.

POST-PRODUCTION

## 29 August 2004

Razor-end nerves showing the film to my family for the first time. I felt acutely alert to any and every reaction, wanting to watch with them but simultaneously wanting to hide away.

They have very informed and positive notes, all of which I will try to find solutions to in the coming week. The 'look' from Ralph at the funeral in which he thinks he sees Lauren and Harry dancing together in the long grass provokes the most reaction, and reiterates Liza's feeling that seeing this couple 'reunited' in his imagination feels like a terrible betrayal of Ruby and needs to be cut.

Very pleased that they both endorsed the excision of the priest shenanigans and the safari scenes. Have not had word from my mother since posting her the script some weeks ago and have begun to dread the worst, so am pretty gobsmacked by her positive response when she phones, saying that she thinks the script is wonderful. I'd never dared believe she would be so enthusiastic, seeing that our proper rapprochement had only come about a few years back.

Isabelle calls to tell me not to come back to Paris as the Avid machines have a virus, which they hope to have fixed by Tuesday. This leaves me free to take the first edited version to composer Pat Doyle at his office in Shepperton Studios. He advises me to listen, ponder and experiment with *everything* people say after seeing it, and only act upon specifics if the same point keeps feeding back. His main note after watching it is to insert more shots of the African landscape, to give it size and afford breathing space, especially after very emotional scenes, and suggests we start the film with a wide exterior shot to give the audience the chance to adjust to where the story is set. Ironic, as this was how the script started, until I was persuaded by Pierre Aïm to open on the back seat of the car with the sleeping Ralph. I'll have to go through all the second-unit car footage to see if we can put together an opening sequence as Pat suggests. His other notes about the timing of particular scenes is invaluably informed by the fact that he is a brilliant raconteur and composer *and* used to be an actor, so he knows how a scene should work from the inside out.

He *hated* the classical temp music I had used, saying that it slowed things down and that *everything* would be transformed and unified with *his* bespoke score. Pat is very emotional and passionate about *everything* and *speaks* in *italics*.

### 1 September 2004

Discussed all the feedback notes with Isabelle and Liza. Immediately set to work trying out new cuts and finding a way to start the film using the car snaking through the landscape. I'm very grateful at this moment to Charlie Watson for being so insistent on getting as much second-unit footage of cars and landscape as possible. It has proved a godsend and enabled an entire opening-credit sequence to be salvaged and created.

MC's new assistant, Laetitia, calls to inform me that she has been in contact with Malcolm McDowell's agent about the clip from *A Clockwork Orange*, and that she is doubtful the Kubrick estate will grant permission. We already have permission from Warner Brothers and are still awaiting clearance from the Kubrick estate, and need to get Malcolm's consent. I call Robert Altman in New York, as he had recently directed Malcolm in *The Company*. Kind and helpful as ever, he offers to track Malcolm down in Russia where he is filming and put me in touch with him directly. 'How's it going otherwise?' he asked. 'Pretty good,' I say, 'except for the producer,' to which he spews, 'They're *all* *\$@%! Hang on in there.'

Bruno phones to say that we need to either cut our edit time down by another week or work six-day weeks, to which Isabelle retorts that we have already reduced the running time considerably and are on our third version after a total of two weeks, which in her experience is as fast as it gets. The flea starts jumping all over the place to get us to edit faster, concerned that the sound studio at Luc Besson's complex in Normandy has been booked and cannot be changed. Isabelle calls the studio direct and discovers that the booking has *not yet* been confirmed. We have consequently lost our slot in the small studio, and will have to use the newly built big studio. Dean Humphreys has repeatedly advised against this as new studios always have technical teething problems and our film would be only the second to guinea-pig in there.

### 3 September 2004

Having sent the video of the latest edit to MC last Friday, it has taken her almost a week to respond. She does so by phone to Isabelle: make the film *longer*, extend the safari and 'cuddle puddle' scenes and cut the deathbed line, 'I never stopped loving your mother.' So now she wants a longer film, having ordered that the script be cut by fifteen pages, the shooting schedule be cut by a week, and another week cut from the editing schedule.

Avid breaks down. Go for lunch on my own and take a long walk to clear my head.

Chris Curling calls from London to confirm that MC has finally agreed to a meeting with Scion next week to sort out the DCMS requirements.

## 4 September 2004

Avid repair takes up most of the morning. Having slimmed the film down to 99 minutes, the reinstatement of scenes and extensions of key emotional moments has quickly pushed it up to 108. Isabelle reassures me that this contraction/expansion is absolutely normal – a precise parallel to the rewriting process.

At Isabelle's behest, and in a nod to MC's demand, we remove Harry's deathbed confession and plan to test it out on my family this weekend. I know this is the Disney soft option, but agree to show willing.

Bruno arrives to discuss dates, saying that we need to complete editing by 14 September, and for some reason seems unable to look any of us in the eye. This means I will have had a total of one month in which to edit the whole film. Isabelle says he will be lucky if we complete by the end of the month and points out that we are already working at great speed. Bruno also announces that he has contracted a French automated dialogue replacement editor to do all the actors' post-sync lines in the studio (to rerecord dialogue where there are noise problems on the original recording due to planes, wind, engines or whatever). Again this seems to me to be in direct contravention of the DCMS requirements, and, more importantly, it doesn't make sense – the film is in English, the actors are English and they all live in London.

The edit process is so all-consuming that it's very difficult to switch off. I waver between feeling I might just have gotten away with it and wanting to throw myself in the Seine.

# POST-PRODUCTION

## 5 September 2004

Tony Frewin emails me in London, confirming that Mrs Kubrick has given her blessing and permission to use the clip from *A Clockwork Orange*, which is a first and a real cinematic coup.

Go round to Gary Williamson's and Chrissie Baker's house to fetch my puppets and other props, and watch the 108-minute edit with them. Possibly because they are so enthused, laughing and crying in all the right places, I feel genuinely moved by my own story for the first time. Their endorsement – and especially eighteen-year-old Will's, who had never read the script – restore my faith in the film.

The removal of the deathbed line weakens the end, though, and having tried without it, it has to be reinstated. The new opening-credit sequence has transformed and properly locates the story. Works a treat.

Chrissie reveals that during the *Camelot* week, when her team were working from 4 a.m. till 11 p.m., she asked MC if it was possible to pay them a little extra for the insane hours they were working to make the schedule. MC sent Martin Jaubert over to negotiate, who very reluctantly agreed to fork out £200 per person, totalling £600.

## 6 September 2004

Back to Paris and the coalface of showbiz. The Avid machines have failed to save some of the edits we did last week. Bruno is called in yet again to try and salvage the situation. Whilst waiting, Liza and Isabelle watch the video of the 108-minute version – not a laugh, titter or sound throughout. It felt like watching *Gone With the Wind* in Mongolian.

## 7 September 2004

Gratefully call my daughter, who is about to start her GCSE year at school, having watched the TV news reporting the abject horror of the Beslan massacre in Russia. Walked to work in a grey daze.

Isabelle has invited an editor friend of hers to come and give us his unvarnished view. I prepared myself for a non-reaction to the humour, as his English is very poor. Not a flicker. While his notes are highly intellectual and serious, some of them prompt us to re-examine scenes we have left untouched for a while, and further streamline others. Isabelle is anxious that we see the current edit on a big screen, preferably with a small audience. Scion readily agree to screen it in London next week, Monday the 13th, so that we have feedback from an English audience. Isabelle requests that Loma Nasha also screen it in Paris on the same day. Bruno says that it can only be shown next Wednesday, the 15th, followed swiftly by a faxed refusal from MC to show it in London before the 20th. This would leave us only four days to respond to the feedback and implement the final changes before the picture is 'locked off'. The editors are incredulous at the delay in test screenings intended to improve the edit.

Scion retort that she has no right to veto any showing and to go ahead. However, MC is still arguing about the DCMS requirements and is going to London tomorrow with a lawyer to fight her corner. Then Bruno calls to announce that there will be no DVD copy of the latest edit for me to take to London this weekend, and that the ADR sound work *will* be done in France by a Frenchman.

Ten minutes later Bruno is back on the line informing us that *all* the sound editing, ADR and mixing *has* to be done in England by Englishmen. You couldn't make this up!

### 9 September 2004

Dean Humphreys lankily breezed in for a visit, full of bonhomie. He's had a meeting with MC to discuss terms – at which she gave him her well-rehearsed 'victim-producer' speech in order to beat down his asking price.

Eclair Studios and Bruno have somehow managed between them to lose a reel of unseen film, and blame Swazi airport customs.

### 14 September 2004

Having never sent me a single note on the script, apart from the order to cut an unspecified fifteen pages before shooting began, MC faxed over a slew of notes yesterday, the majority of which make me wonder whether she has ever properly understood the screenplay. Mercifully Isabelle dismissed most of them with a wave of her hand.

We take the phone off the hook and switch off all mobiles in an attempt to work without interference, and have a very good day – laughter has returned to our little edit room. Isabelle is understandably keen to keep relations with MC as neutral as she can. Before we leave at 9 p.m., she responds to MC's multiple phone messages and reassures her that we have indeed acted upon and implemented *some* of her notes.

### 15 September 2004

The established rhythm of editing all week, making a copy on Friday afternoons and screening it at home over the weekend is disrupted by the requirement to hold a midweek screening solely for MC. As there will be no audience from which to gauge reactions, it will be of no use to me whatsoever, so I decide not to attend. I take off and see *The Bourne Identity*, in which Matt Damon is chased around a very wintry Europe by guns and a pounding soundtrack.

### 16 September 2004

As I wasn't there to receive MC's notes after the screening, she apparently went into a rant, threatening she would stop the edit. Ahhhh, that would teach me who was the producer of the film.

I called her and said she could come over immediately. Which she did, and demanded to know why her suggestions and cuts had not been implemented. Isabelle calmly explained that *every* take of *every* scene was discussed at length, and as editor she had chosen to ignore some of her suggestions as the knock-on effect would unbalance the scenes which followed. MC remained hell-bent on the removal of the deathbed line, and demanded that I write an alternative for Gabriel to post-sync.

Her eyes popped when I casually asked what she intended doing about the missing reel of film. Maybe Bruno had not mentioned this to her . . .

### 17 September 2004

Edit aborted! Reason given: MC says the South African bank and co-producing partners have withheld funds. I suspect she was aware of this at her screening two days ago and knew the edit had to stop anyway.

Isabelle points out that they have received not a word of consolation or concern from their 'producer' about their work and pay being halted three-quarters of the way through. It seems to have been assumed that both editors will stay attached to the film no matter how long the shut-down. Liza predicts this will last a week, Isabelle has no idea and I opt for ten days.

Although MC seems to fear that if the film goes to London it will somehow be taken away from her, I insist that I be allowed to screen the film there next week so that I can make use of the time wasted by the edit shut-down. She reluctantly agrees, and I insist that she phone Bruno there and then to guarantee that I get a video copy in time.

### 20 September 2004

First proper screening at the De Lane Lea studios in Dean Street, Soho. Co-producers Chris Curling and Phil Robinson, the sound team Grahame Peters and Andy Walker (colleagues of Dean Humphreys from their Crossfade sound company), casting team Celestia and Alex, Gary the designer, Karen our script supervisor, close friends and the veteran editor Mike Ellis – whom I had initially approached to edit the film until told I had to use a French person – are all there.

It went much better than I anticipated and everyone seemed to be surprised at how few notes they had to offer. I religiously wrote down every single opinion, most of which I agreed with – plot clarification that can easily be sorted out by the insertion of a few post-sync lines, plus areas requiring adjustment that Isabelle and I had in hand.

### 21 September 2004

Isabelle reports on the Paris screening, to which twenty English speakers were recruited via the consulate (!) and handed question-naires, which MC took at the end. She repeated to Isabelle that she wanted the safari scene reinstated and the deathbed line excised. Over *my* dead body!

### 22 September 2004

Second London screening at Mr Young's cinema. Packed with ICM agents, novelist Kathy Lette, producer Barnaby Thompson, Victoria Wood and Peter Capaldi, plus other curious and willing friends. It was the *perfect* test screening. They laughed and they cried and, even if *slightly* partisan, they totally restored my confidence after the nonsense of last week. Their notes identified the same problems as the first screening, confirming how invaluable this process is at this crucial stage of the edit. Isabelle warned that although it might be brutal, it is obviously better to get feedback when there is still time to rectify and address the faults, rather than after the film is locked off and you are stuck with an 'if only' fait accompli.

Met Jeff Abberley and Chris Curling at the Scion office in the afternoon, who said the Paris screening was a disaster, with not an audible reaction throughout. Chris says that MC *thinks* the edit will restart on 11 October, which will in turn delay the sound mix and studio bookings. What cannot be delayed is the post-sync ADR dialogue session booked with Emily Watson this Saturday at Twickenham studios, as she is due to leave for Australia to start shooting another film the next day.

Bruno, who is foot-soldiering over to see Dean Humphreys in Twickenham on MC's behalf, calls Dean three times to check how to get there from Waterloo.

### 25 September 2004

Twickenham studios. Emily recreates sections of her performance to eradicate the sound glitches with immaculate timing and professionalism. What a sea-change to be dealing directly with an actor again after all the post-production frustrations.

### 27 September 2004

A common suggestion from the various screenings is to reduce Lauren's ferocity towards her son Ralph, and keep it specific to her estranged husband Harry. The consensus is that she is too cruel and cold. While the hiatus has afforded time to reflect and reconsider the edit, I'm desperate to get started again. The film revolves around in my head all day long and in my dreams. There is no escape or respite.

## 29 September 2004

Another screening with a proper audience, and one to which Jeff Abberley had invited Isabelle to come over from Paris. Went extremely well – lots of laughs, an audible gasp when Harry puts a gun to Ralph's head, and we could hear people crying at the end.

Both Jeff and Chris Curling, having endured the stony screening in Paris with MC last week, are convinced that what they saw today was a different version – the enthusiasm of the audience response transformed their experience. Mightily encouraging to get emotionally charged responses to the film first hand, as opposed to producer input. Isabelle is particularly taken with how an English audience responds so positively to it.

MC calls her, and says that the edit will not restart until 11 October and that we will have only a week in which to complete it!

## 30 September 2004

Jeff Abberley comes up with a plan to restart the edit in London on Monday the 4th, deliver a new cut on the 11th, screen it for a 'warm' audience of known people, followed by a 'cold' screening with people no one knows and who know nothing about the film. He offers to pay for the hard discs to be shipped over from Paris at his expense to prevent the delay.

### 1 October 2004

MC vetoes this plan outright.

### 6 October 2004

Spent all day at Shepperton with composer Pat Doyle discussing ideas, and listening to him sketching in themes on his keyboard as the latest cut of the film spooled forth. The great news is that the London Symphony Orchestra have agreed to record the finished score and are booked in.

Pat is the funniest man I have ever had the pleasure of working with, fuelled by a combination of Celtic rage, a sublime sense of the absurd and irreverence in the face of anything smacking of self-aggrandizement. He is incapable of doing anything by half measures – his passions and hatreds blast in every direction with equal force. His producer anecdotes cheer me up no end and are pretty much on a par with how people generally talk about estate agents. His advice is 'stick to your vision, *you* wrote and directed this film, not them'.

### 11 October 2004

The edit restarted in Paris without me as I was on Argos duty filming an advert in London. Isabelle made all the new cuts and a multitude of tiny adjustments, reducing the film back down to 99 minutes. I watched it when I got back, judging it to be ninety per cent improved, grateful that the screenings in London during the enforced hiatus had proved so useful.

Bruno spent the entire morning transferring all the post-sync dialogue we did in London last week into the Avid, whilst we sat around and waited, wondering why the fuck he didn't do it when the machines were standing idle.

At Isabelle's urging, I reluctantly agreed to go to a screening of the latest cut with MC present. The sound system was duff, and there was a gruesome lack of response for the entire 99 minutes, followed by her 'notes'. I wrote down her 'pearls' with all the vigour of a dead man. They boiled down to cuts suggested by some bloke from a French TV station – like I give a continental what he should think. I told her that I have not made this film to please a TV executive. She blathered on about the time-lapse montage between younger and older Ralph needing to be cut, and privately told Isabelle that she still wants *all* of *Camelot* cut out – I suspect to save the song-rights costs. Oh, and just for a change, she wants the deathbed line to come out.

When I asked whether she was coming for the two London test screenings with proper audiences, she declined, saying she had a very important meeting; if she did she'd come face to face with people who still hadn't been paid! Isabelle insisted we instigate her changes and those of the Brits to show that we are willing, and take the opportunity of testing them with an audience.

### 14 October 2004

Edit all morning in a state of barely suppressed rage, feeling like a traitor to my own cause.

Isabelle suggests that the reason MC wants the *Camelot* scenes cut might be because there is no musical tradition in French cinema – it is the one country where *Mary Poppins*, *The Sound of Music*, *Moulin*

*Rouge* and *Chicago* all failed at the box office. The four minutes of screen time taken up with *Camelot* in my film hardly qualify as a musical, but I suppose it goes some way to explaining why she is so hell-bent on removing them, although I believe it's also to do with the song copyright costs.

Haul myself off to Pierre Kubel's office to see the production stills for the first time as they have refused to let them leave the building! Kubel runs an operation that reconfigures American poster campaigns for the French market. MC swoops in and launches into her full Lady Muck routine, barking orders to assistants. Whilst sifting through the piles of hitherto unseen stills, I ask her when the crew are likely to get paid, to which she blames the Rand Merchant Bank for the delay. *Plus ça change!*

### 15 October 2004

Caught the Eurostar to London last night, for the final test screenings and a meeting with the Works sales company to discuss their ideas for artwork and brochures for the imminent American Film Market sales convention. They were very accommodating of my abhorrence for all things sepia, and agreed to replace the *Passage to India*-style tinted photos of Emily with a sexier image.

Jeff Abberley casually drops the little bombshell that MC intends calling the film *Fatherland* in France, despite the fact that such a film already exists and, coincidentally, also stars Miranda Richardson.

*Highest priority* email from Valerie Lindon, the music supervisor in Paris. Despite my having been informed by MC in April that Valerie had cleared all song permissions – at thirty per cent less, apparently, than would have been the case had it been done in London – Valerie now says that the source-music budget has gone way over, and that I have to choose alternative, cheap songs, and questions whether I really need all the source music anyway. She suggests that Pat Doyle composes some 'period' pastiche songs in lieu of the original recordings. To lay this scenario at my door in the last days before the film is locked off seems to me nothing less than barking.

Deep breathing required not to let this spoil the 4 p.m. screening, where I'm very glad to see the friendly faces of Alan Rickman, John Fraser, Rod Goodlife, Paul Weilland, Dean Humphreys, Grahame Peters, Andy Walker, Deborah Moore, Simon Greenaway and Sid Mitchell amongst the audience for this 97-minute version, the shortest it's ever been.

The 6.30 screening has two welcome familiar faces in Meera Syal and Sanjeev Bhaskar amongst the 'recruited' punters who none of us knew and who knew nothing about the film. The English co-producers fill up the back row and look apprehensive. The film plays to pin-drop silence when it should, laughter in between and tears at the end – the whole gamut. Rather than hand out a questionnaire, I field questions about everything. The main thrust of them are to do with the speed of the film, with a unanimous vote to extend sequences.

Jeff Abberley has the good grace to concede that it would be an improvement to reinstate another three minutes back into the film. Feel triumphant and exonerated and grateful for this U-turn regarding key sequences. I suspect he assumed the audience would never have demanded a longer version. The contentious deathbed line was also unanimously endorsed, bar one dissenter, who was summarily shouted down!

Julie Walters had snuck in, having just wrapped another film, and piped up that 'The truth is the truth – don't mess with it.' She said that on *Educating Rita* there was a notion to have her and Michael Caine go off together at the end. The fact that they didn't was what made the film end so poignantly. The audience applauded their agreement.

I feel vindicated and ready to return to attend to the finishing touches prior to locking the picture down.

Beautiful email from John Fraser who says that 'a messed up childhood is the greatest gift any creative artist could have – and you are the living proof of it'.

### 18 October 2004

Return to Paris for the final week's edit, determined to deliver the film *I* can live with and feel proud about. With a running time of less than 105 minutes, I have final cut.

### 19 October 2004

Three days left to edit and every producer and co-producer is choking to deliver their last phone book's worth of notes via email, fax, telephone and Pepe the donkey.

I reply in reassuring generalizations, promising to try and please all sides as best we can. It is the only chance I have of getting a good night's sleep.

### 20 October 2004

All quiet – no calls, notes, threats, pleadings or interruptions. Almost manage to complete the day without obstruction, until the flea itches over, demanding a copy of the latest cut for MC.

After tinkering with a plethora of notes and changes, the running time is now back to 99 minutes, which is precisely the same length as the screenplay. One page has, after all, equalled one minute of screen time.

We feel we have reached as good a compromise as we are able.

*22 October 2004*

Final screening on the TV set in our little edit room. Pierre Aïm attended, seeing the film for the first time. Liz Crowther, who is studying at Jacques Le Coq mime school, was also invited. Both were very complimentary and endorsed the deathbed line. Again I was amazed at how the presence of an audience, even if it's only two people, can totally transform the experience of watching the film – our senses are razor sharp, elephant-eared to every response, shuffle, inhalation, itch, laugh and tear.

After they left, we made our final, *final* tweaks and adjustments and then by mutual agreement decided that we were ready to 'sign off' and make video and beta copies (for cinema screenings) for me to take home to give to the sound guys and Pat Doyle.

Went round the corner to the bistro that we have frequented over the past seven weeks for our last lunch, and I gave Isabelle and Liza hampers full of their favourite goodies from Le Grand Epicerie. We all felt very emotional, having gone through such an intense process together. Isabelle was amazed that we have managed to edit the film so quickly, given the interruptions and hiatus. All three of us cried when we parted – I will always be indebted to both these ladies for their loyalty, patience and professionalism, and for teaching me how to edit.

Eurostar'd to London to an empty house. My wife is in Cape Town and my daughter is on a school trip to Thailand. Weekend break before the sound edit begins on Monday.

## 25 October 2004

No sooner has the visual edit completed than the whole process starts all over again on the sound – to Crossfade sound company at Twick-enham Studios owned by Dean Humphreys, Grahame Peters and Andy Walker.

We watch the film and they take notes of where and what sound effects I am after. It's strangely anti-climactic having been so pres-sured to complete the picture edit, and odd to be in such a blokey set-up after the femininities of Paris. I'm sent home in the afternoon and told that they will call me in every now and again to check each reel as they complete the sound effects, but essentially I am redun-dant for a while.

Flopped about like a seal in search of some playmates.

## 12 November 2004

Shepperton Studios. Go through the score with Pat Doyle, Maggie Rodford and MC. Frugal formalities, then Pat launches forth with a live rendition on his synthesizer of every music cue, punctuated with a veritable fan dance of explanations and enthusings about his musical ideas and themes.

After this great display, MC bleeps in a flat monotone that she thinks 'it's good', and says nothing else.

I said to her, 'I hear you intend changing the title of the film in France to *Fatherland*.'

She averts her eyes and mumbles, 'This has not been decided yet.' Then there is a barrage of questions from me about when the sound and music people will get paid. Pat and Maggie have told me that they will not allow any of the music 'elements' to leave London until payment has been made as per their contracts.

She says that she is working on the money issues every minute of the day.

'Well, that's your job – you're the producer.'

### 22 November 2004

I got a letter from someone I was at school with who has tracked me down via a website:

> The reason I am writing is that I found out about your film on the internet and saw that one of the characters was called Gwen. I guess that you have changed the names of many of the characters and that Gwen is a made-up name as well? However, there were not that many people called Gwen in Swaziland at the time, so I am hoping there is nothing about the character that would upset my mum, Gwen. She made the costumes for *Camelot* and was not actually in it, though dad was a knight. They are both still alive and well and living in rural Worcestershire. I hope you can understand why I am a little concerned when I read about your Gwen. It would be nice to have some reassurance before the film opens so that she does not get any nasty surprises.

I duly wrote reassurances that she is not in the story at all and that it is not an historical documentary but a drama. No doubt this issue will rear its head again many times, as it did during the shooting. Everyone has their own ideas as to who the characters are based on.

### *24 November 2004*

Dean Humphreys calls to report that Bruno has asked him to accept delayed payment – which Dean has refused as he has yet to be paid *anything*. Dean double-checks that, as agreed, the final sound mix, i.e. post-Normandy, would be completed at Twickenham Studios after 17 December. Bruno announces that this will never happen, that all the sound will be done in France, and to ignore what Jeff Abberley and Chris Curling say. Dean is then called by MC herself, this time trying to persuade him to defer half his fee. He stuck to his guns saying his payment is contractually due this Friday at the latest, and that he would refer this mess to Jeff Abberley to sort out.

'But you will come to do the mix in Normandy?'

'When you've paid, yes.'

### *25 November 2004*

Dean is called again by MC, who claims she has no money to pay him. As if Dean should give a flying fuck.

Maggie Rodford, meanwhile, has told her in 'the politest of terms' that unless she is fully paid as per her contract, the music will simply be withheld until such time as she was able to pay. Surprise surprise, Maggie is rewarded with full payment, albeit two weeks late. Dean knows all this and is deaf to MC's claims of destitution.

With less than two days before the soundtrack score recording, Valerie Lindon emails the list of songs she has chosen to replace the original choices, which are modern cover versions of songs I'd never heard of, along with a repeated proviso that 'Patrick Doyle write something to fit'. In yer dreams, lady!

Never giving up, MC phones Dean again to try and get him to agree to the deferment of half his fee. By the end of the day, Dean having refused to accept this, Scion agree to pay the 'missing' half and save her arse.

### 27 November 2004

Air Studios, Hampstead, with the London Symphony Orchestra, no less. Punctual start at 2 p.m. under the baton of conductor-orchestrator James Shearman. They are as disciplined and precise as a Swiss watch factory. Twenty-nine musicians magically make it sound like a Wagnerian 110-piece. Absolutely thrilling to be standing there watching the opening credits of my film enhanced, engulfed and transformed by a live orchestra playing Pat's haunting, evocative score. The slightest adjustment is instantly incorporated and they play the score as though they have done so all their lives, rather than for the first time this afternoon. Whereas an actor might anticipate murmurs of approbation or applause on delivering an extraordinary speech, the musicians show no emotion and listen silently to the conductor for his notes, before diving straight back in again.

The tea breaks are taken on the dot, and the orchestra reconvene equally precisely. They break at five for supper, come back at six and complete at two minutes to nine. Many compliments are paid to Pat for his beautiful score.

## 30 November 2004

Yesterday and the day before were spent in Air-Edel Studios off Baker Street, for an epic mixing session with a fleet of engineers (all of whom were called Nick), Pat Doyle and Maggie Rodford.

Dean calls and says our trip to Normandy is cancelled, as he hasn't been paid. Bruno says this will hold up post-production. Dean's simple retort is 'When you pay, we play.' Bruno finally squeaks that he will be paid by 3 December. I, meanwhile, will not get another bean, after the 'deferment' deal a couple of weeks prior to shooting.

Listened to Pat's score all day – by turns melancholic, wistful, nostalgic, urgent, lyrical and gorgeously romantic. Sent him a case of his favourite red wine to thank him.

## 4 December 2004

Summoned to a casting call for *Pirates of the Caribbean II* and *III*. Knowing that they have already seen Bill Nighy, Iain Glenn and Jim Broadbent, and will doubtless choose the brilliant and idiosyncratic Bill if he is available, leaves me wondering whether I should even bother going, but having been out of the acting loop for so long, I know I should be grateful for the chance to be a ponce-for-hire again.

The anticipation of humiliation trickles down my spine. There is no script as yet, so decisions will be based entirely on first impressions and/or your suitability as a stop-gap in case the bloke who's already been offered it falls through. Not that I am entirely cynical – it's just that I'm not sure how much longer I can take having to do the old verbal soft-shoe shuffle for our American Movie Masters and hear the familiar patter of 'Man, we love your work, you're soooo talented and we're sooooo excited!'

The producers and director are as pleasantly informal and friendly in a way English people are rarely capable of being on first meeting, but every second I banter back and forth, I know I haven't a gnat in hell's chance of getting this role. I go through the motions, as do they, concluding with the time-honoured 'we'll be in touch' kiss off.

I'd always thought this process would get easier with age and experience, but the reverse is true. You just get better at reading the concealed rejection between the lines of what they say. The kinder they are, the quicker they'd like you to dissolve into the floor.

Check my emails – and Jeff Abberley has copied me in on his correspondence with MC in which she states that she is going to Normandy on Wednesday to 'push for cutting "The Lusty Month of May" ' song from *Camelot* as the rights are still not resolved!

My blood pressure rockets north.


## 6 December 2004

At 11.30 last night I arrived at Luc Besson's studios stuck in the middle of nowhere in Normandy, after a seven-and-a-half-hour train and car journey. It was as cold and misty as witches' breath. Dean Humphreys and his assistant Nick Lowe had kindly waited up. Mercifully, there was no sign of Bruno.

The studio complex is housed in a series of vast barns in the grounds of a chateau, and the exterior gives no clue to the massive state-of-the-art screen and mixing desks within. Within five minutes of sitting down, we are told there are technical problems booting the computers. A flurry of very young techno-fiends appear from nowhere, and watching them, I realize that they are clones of the guys at school who always volunteered to do the lighting or sound for plays.

Two hours later, we finally get started. Dean's and Nick's experience and professionalism mean we make good progress mixing the dialogue, sound effects and music score together, and we work through till 9 p.m. Really satisfying to get a run at these combined elements and gain a proper sense of what the final film will be like.

## 7 December 2004

Rattle ahead through the morning and break for lunch at 1 p.m. This is a monastic, all-male world of technicians, apart from the female maître d' in the dining room. Nearly choke on my last mouthful when chief technician, Fabrice, comes over to announce that due to further computer problems, all the work we have done this morning has been wiped out and cannot be retrieved. Dean's warning that new studios always have technical breakdowns was painfully prescient. There is flurry of calls to computer experts in Paris and Switzerland, which delays everything. Work late in order to redo all the lost work of the morning.

The flea and MC are visiting tomorrow. My wife has advised me to avoid confrontation at all costs.

## 8 December 2004

Start work promptly at 9 a.m. Two hours later they arrive and plonk down at the back of the theatre without a peep. At lunch MC corners Dean, demanding to know why we haven't stopped work to show her the completed reels. Dean says that the decision as to who sees what, and when, is the director's prerogative, not his.

Back at the mixing desk after lunch the wretched machine crashes again. In the ensuing technical flap I hear MC leaving frantic messages for Maggie Rodford to call her back about the outcome of the *Camelot*-rights debacle. I presume she is hoping to have a final costing maybe with which to justify why I have to make further changes, despite the fact that we are in the middle of mixing the final version.

I phone Maggie, who confirms that MC is desperately trying to get the song-rights scenario settled. Valerie Lindon's reluctance to withdraw from the Warner Chappell negotiations and allow the London office to deal with them has resulted in an impasse.

During yet another breakdown, Dean says she collared him outside and declared that as she has to leave by 5 p.m., she has to see the first completed mixed reels. Dean said, 'I'm not being Swiss [God love him], but be it Spielberg or Scorsese, Polanski or Richard E. Grant, this is the director's call.'

'Yes, but I'm the *producer*.'

I expected the wheels to come off her trolley, and Dean and Nick speculated that whilst we are still mixing in the coming week, she will probably move heaven and earth to get the song-rights costings concluded and then make her final push to remove music to save money before the final Dolby mix is done.

At 5.45 p.m. MC and the flea escape through the back door without a word. Given the circumstances, I was pleased to have managed to be similarly silent to them all day, other than a curt 'Morning' when they arrived.

Chris Curling calls to see how we were progressing, and comforts me by saying that the later she leaves everything, the better for me, as any moment now it will be too late for changes without incurring further costs. His advice: 'Hang in there.'

Throughout dinner, Dean – who is an excellent mimic – keeps peppering his conversation with a squeaky 'But I'm the *producer*' . . .

# POST-PRODUCTION

## *9 December 2004*

No computer problems and we actually get a *whole* day's work done. Maggie Rodford calls at 3 p.m. with 'cautious good news' – that MC has officially asked her to take over the music negotiations and instructed Lindon to withdraw completely. It turns out that no alternative rights have been negotiated in the past two months, so the songs already in the film will stay.

Maggie assures me that the rights will be settled, but not prior to the final Dolby recording, meaning that in order to change anything, MC would have to spend a pile to reopen the mix after it's been completed.

I think that seals it, and she'll have to pay for the songs already in the film. Nobody can say they weren't given fair warning: these songs were in the script from day one . . .

Bruno calls at 5 p.m. saying that MC wants to see the film next Wednesday in Paris. Dean thinks we will finish the mix by tomorrow evening, Friday, giving us time to have a final, *final* screening to triple-check everything on Monday morning, and be ready to record the Dolby that afternoon. This news sent Bruno into a tail spin of Vicky Pollard yeah-but-no-but-yeah-buts, and he let slip that this won't give the producer a chance to make changes.

Dean repeats that we will have done the Dolby by then, and by doing so will have saved a week's studio rental, which is a substantial cost. You can almost hear the synaptic crackle and pop in the ether as Bruno's brain computes this morsel. I immediately tell Jeff Abberley and Chris Curling that we are ready to complete. 'It's in your court, Jeff – delay the Dolby, or save a week's studio rental.'

Dean and Nick work into the night to get ahead. The Independence sequence reveals Dean's considerable expertise, as he mixes the crowds, choirs, cars, chanting, brass band, music score et al. into a harmonious whole. At midnight he tells me that, 'In all my experience of mixing sound on films, this has been the fastest I've ever done it and you have been an absolute joy to work with.' I nearly fall over.

### 10 December 2004

2.45 p.m., the final reel is mixed and we are ready to shut up shop. Dean calls Bruno to inform him and get confirmation that we will Dolby on Monday after our screening.

'But the Dolby man cannot come on Monday, Dean.'

'Oh yes he can, Bruno, I already called him. We worked together on *The Pianist*. I have booked him to come on Monday afternoon.'

### 12 December 2004

Jeff copies me in on the email from MC in which she claims the music budget has bloated so astronomically that she *has* to make song cuts. Bruno texts Dean to say that the Dolby will be delayed after all, presumably as authorized by Jeff and MC.

### 13 December 2004

The technical gremlins have descended again. Reel five has distorted and has to be completely re-recorded, then the *whole* mixing desk goes phut at 1 p.m. Most reels recorded last week are now 'corrupted' and will have to be redone. The French technical guys don't know where to look or what to say.

5.10 p.m. on what should have been the last day of sound mixing, and it remains uncompleted. Dean takes the executive decision to abort – the computer system has completely broken down and the engineers have no idea how long it will take to rectify. He has agreed to return and re-record everything from scratch on his own when the system is repaired. There is nothing we can do in Normandy, so we all return to England.

So MC will get her Wednesday screening after all.

### 15 December 2004

Jeff emails all parties to confirm that 'the final cut of the film . . . must not be changed by anyone. I will not accept any additions or any deletions'.

I send an email to the flea:

Bruno – get this into your head – I will not be coming back to Normandy for the mix until I am guaranteed my final cut will not be messed with – no songs will be cut. Your producer told Chris Curling that she reserved the right to re-open the Dolby in January and make changes to the music if she wanted to without my consent. Jeff Abberley has emailed his insistence that nothing can be cut or changed. Until the music issues have been settled, there will be no final sound mix.

Then I email MC:

I have just spoken to Jeff who confirmed that he told you last week that none of the music could be changed. I was called this afternoon by Bruno informing me about getting on a train to Normandy. I will not do anything until I am guaranteed that the music will be left wholly intact . . . Do not think you can get away with trying to persuade Dean to complete the sound mix without me – he has all the sound stems [the separate components – dialogue, music and sound effects – that combine to make the finished soundtrack], effects and music back in London. You do not own this film. You do not have the authority to overrule my final cut. You do not have the courage to return calls, answer emails, confront problems head on . . .

Her two-word reply actually made me laugh:

You're welcome.

### 16 December 2004

5.45 p.m. conference call. Chris Curling and Scion co-producer/ lawyer Julia Blackman want me to return to Normandy. I say that I will, the moment I have it in writing that MC will not change any of the music.

Felt awful having to be so insistent with them, as they have been so wonderfully supportive throughout.

### 17 December 2004

Julia Blackman emails MC mid-morning to confirm that the mix should be finalized without any music changes and that 'Richard will be happy to complete once you have agreed to these terms by return.' She does so, but only after stating how unprofessional it has been of me 'to take the film hostage'. I laugh out loud and long, and readily agree to return to Normandy to complete on Monday with Dean.

## 20 December 2004

Loma Nasha office calls claiming that Dean and I should pay for our Eurostar tickets in London as it's too late to post them. When we arrive in Paris, it transpires that the driver doesn't have either a clue or a map to get us to Normandy. Finally crawl into Besson's studio compound around midnight. We try to laugh, but our jaw muscles have cramped by the time we get there.

## 21 December 2004

Dean gets into the studio at 7 a.m. to repair the sound stems. At 9.30 – and again I try to laugh – the computer crashes. The public-relations lady cruises by to ask Dean if he would recommend the studio and work there again; he diplomatically said he would. I suspect the look on my face deters her from asking me.

Joy Wong at the Works sales company emails the news that the film has not been selected for the Berlin Film Festival. Gutted.

The Dolby engineer is keen to start the master recording, and is scheduled to begin at 2.30. Bruno appears at 2.27 and announces that the completed Dolby disc cannot return to London with Dean tonight, announcing that it 'belongs to Loma Nasha'. Dean orders the recording be aborted whilst Scion are called to deal with this. The impasse concludes with MC now saying she only wants a copy of the disc, and as soon as it's made, she will send the original to London.

Dean and I leave empty-handed, but not before he gets a verbal promise from Bruno that the wretched disc would be couriered to London tomorrow afternoon so that he can complete his work before Christmas. 'I shan't hold my breath,' he says.

It's over. Not with a Berlin bang, but a Normandy whisper. Despite this, I have managed to keep in the deathbed line, the *Camelot* songs and the source music, and got the film completed pretty much as I'd wanted.

'Feel proud' is Dean's sage advice.

### 24 December 2004

Christmas Eve, and at the last minute, the Dolby disc was delivered to Dean at Twickenham Studios. The 'simple' matter of inserting the opening titles and end credits and colour grading the film is the final hurdle prior to the film being delivered to the sales company. Bruno emails a schedule with the end of January tagged for the first colour-graded test print and credits.

### 25 January 2005

Email from Jeff Abberley: Johnnie Walker have refused permission for their product to be shown on screen for the following reasons: Gabriel Byrne plays a drunk and is clearly drinking their whisky; his scenes represent irresponsible drinking; the character he plays would not be classed as suitable for the representation of their product. They have strongly advised that the scene be removed. If it isn't, they may enforce legal action.

No prizes for guessing who told production designer Gary Williamson months ago to leave these clearances with her and not to worry about them. The only solution is to replace the labels digitally with a fake alternative. Much wrangling between Paris and London follows, Loma Nasha claiming it can be done much more cheaply in France. Yeah, like the song rights. Takes a couple of days to get them to agree to the London deal, and on it goes.

### February to April 2005

The credits have to be finalized and signed off by all the producers before they are filmed and inserted. The majority of the credits are contractual anyway, yet it takes till 2 March for all parties to agree – longer than it took to shoot the film. It seems as if some people don't want this process ever to come to a reasonable conclusion.

Each time I go to Eclair Studios in Paris to watch the print, there are technical breakdowns and I never get to see it from start to finish. More worryingly, in some shots the microphone boom or camera tracks suddenly appear where they hadn't before.

Harry Hook and Peter Capaldi both warned me about the listless melancholy that sets in when it all stops. It's only now that I am knee deep in the stuff that I know precisely what they mean. As hard as I try to galvanize thoughts around doing something new, the nagging undertow of the film still not being finished prevents all forward motion, and I find myself unable to concentrate on anything.

### 26 April 2005

Screening of the answer print, the print that is releasable in a cinema, at Technicolor laboratories opposite Heathrow. Very excited to see the finished colour-graded film.

Even before the title comes up, there are obvious problems – white streaks in the opening credit sequence, water marks, and what looks like a light spray of soot over some of the lettering.

It gets worse. I clock twelve instances where the boom microphone dips into frame, and I feel the familiar dread of having to go into battle yet again.

The current state of the print means that there is insufficient time to produce a new one in time for the Cannes screenings. After a plethora of emails and phone calls, it is established that the print from which Technicolor have been working was dirty all along, and never had a correct framing leader guide, which would have hidden the bobbing boom.

The technical guys shake their heads. The battle will now shift between two labs.

### 5 May 2005

Turned forty-eight. I cannot relate that number to the age I feel inside. I'm reminded of what Sir John Gielgud said when I asked him how old he was, while working with him on Jane Campion's *Portrait of a Lady*: 'Oh, somewhere in my nineties, dear boy, but I am in fact thirty-six, trapped inside this old frame which is falling apart all around me.'

The Works, who are responsible for selling the film, but have refused to take delivery of it in its current state, have diplomatically brought in Neil Meredith from Finishing Post to arbitrate between the two warring labs and give his unbiased, professional opinion of the print. He says it's filthy, and that the projectionist will need to raise the print frame to try and hide the boom.

Turned down by the Cannes Festival committee. There is slight consolation in the fact that no British films got selected, and they passed on *Vera Drake* last year. However, it remains the biggest film market and the Works have booked screenings there next week for buyers and sales agents.

### *11 May 2005*

Yet another visit to the Technicolor lab to see Neil Meredith and identify the ongoing problems with the print. Despite three 'baths', the opening credits are still scratchy, water-marked, and feature intermittent rogue lines. And this is the print that's being screened in Cannes tomorrow night!

Leave with detailed instructions for the French projectionist to reframe the film.

### *12 May 2005*

Eighteen hours in Cannes go like this. Picked up at Nice airport by an old curmudgeon who drove like Nero through the back roads, narrowly avoiding three collisions when he got busy dialling his mobile and forgot to look at the road. Hurtled off to the cinema where the film is being given a dress-rehearsal run to establish the projection problems. Bruno appears. Within five minutes of the film starting, the music sounds as if it's being played on a warped tape machine operated by a drunk. When I ask for it to be stopped and corrected, Bruno says there's nothing wrong with it. I unleash a broadside in which I inform him that unless it is fixed, I will not let the film be shown in this state to professional buyers. He scuttles out and attempts to get it sorted.

It beggars all belief that they can bear for the film to be shown in this state.

Mia Bays, a sales executive from the Works, who has never seen the film, is equally dumbfounded. When it lollops to the end I am reassured by the projectionist and organizers that it will be shown in the adjacent screening room, and will not have these sound problems. MC lurks in the projection box and has the good sense not to come anywhere near me.

Drinks with the team from the Works, and Joy Wong strongly advises me against staying for the screening beyond my short introduction, warning me that it can be very depressing as the buyers leave, walk in and out, chat on their mobiles and so on.

The screening room is packed, and I try to make as funny an introductory speech as I can, saying that I have been warned not to stay for all the reasons given by Joy, which is why I will sit in the front row, so I can't see if any of them walk out. This gets a laugh and the film spools forth, with rectified sound. It also gets laughs, and I can hear people crying at the end. A slew of people come up and pay compliments. The Scion team are clearly relieved and pleased, as am I.

MC seems to have single-handedly alienated the English producers, co-producers and sales team, which exonerates me from any vestige of blame I might have felt for things going AWOL, yet I'm still pretty taken aback when we are all asked to a post-screening party on the Scion boat moored in the harbour and discover that she does not seem to have been invited. That has to hurt bad. The fact that she will have to pay for new titles and an entirely new print is also going to hurt.

### 23 May 2005

Joy Wong calls with the dire news that despite the positive feedback from all the screenings, they have not secured a *single* sale. Felt like I'd been run over. After all that we have gone through, it is *brutal*. Every drink-fuelled insult that my father ever hurled at me tickertapes through my head: '*You are nothing. You are a nobody. You will never amount to anything. You talentless little shit.*'

The shame I feel is burning my skin from the inside out.

## 6 June 2005

We have been chosen to open the Edinburgh Film Festival! *Levitated* – *finally* some good news. I felt an electric current zing round my innards.

## 8 June 2005

Gabriel Byrne emails:

> By the leppin' lamb of the divine Jazes Christ, there'll be an almighty time of it with the whole *Wah-Wah* brigade up there.

Nick Hoult emails:

> That's brilliant news. I'd love to come to Edinburgh. It would be great to c every 1 again. Thank you. *Wah-Wah* was the best time of my short life.

## 9 June 2005

Invitation to the Toronto Film Festival in mid-September. The quandary is that they want it to be the world premiere, which would cancel out Edinburgh. However, we have accepted Scotland already and despite MC's preference for dumping Edinburgh in favour of Toronto, Joy Wong at the Works says we can't do this. The prospect of *two* dates when before we had none is something I am happy to live with till a decision is made.

Hear via Neil Meredith that Loma Nasha have finally started the production of a new print.

### 16 June 2005

A whole week has eked by without word from Toronto, but today they agreed to the world premiere being in Edinburgh. They have offered us a 'special presentation' screening in Canada and *hopefully* these two festivals will secure distribution. This has revived my spirits radically!

### 22 June 2005

Just when I thought the music-rights issues were dead and buried, I am copied into emails between Jeff Abberley and MC, who is now refusing to accept that Warner Chappell in London require full payment for world rights *before* the film is released. She claims that if she went via Warner Chappell in France, they would not require the monies up front. Her obduracy is staggering and makes my blood run cold.

I called Joy Wong at the Works to confirm that as per the delivery deal they have, all rights are to be paid for in advance. Joy diplomatically agrees to send MC a 'casual' email to put this on record.

### 23 June 2005

Technicolor lab to watch the final 'answer' print with Neil Meredith, sent over from Paris. Despite some scratches remaining in the opening credits, the film *finally* looks like a professional print. It's only taken *seven* months to achieve this!

### 17 August 2005

Fly up to Edinburgh for the world premiere. As it's opening the film festival, there is a press conference in the early afternoon, preceded by a mini-cast reunion for Gabriel Byrne, Emily Watson, who is eight months pregnant, Nicholas Hoult, Zac Fox, Julian Wadham, Olivia Grant and Sid Mitchell. Miranda Richardson, Celia Imrie, Julie Walters and Fenella Woolgar are all otherwise engaged.

As pleased as we all obviously are to see each other again, it feels not entirely unlike meeting up with someone you once had a passionate relationship with and now find yourself making small talk with in public. A year has passed since we finished shooting, and Scotland is an unfamiliar context.

There are six screenings this evening, staggered so that we can introduce the cast to each audience. The response to the film is precisely what the doctor ordered: lots of laughter giving way to tears at the end, and resounding applause. Thrilled to get the approbation of Anthony Minghella afterwards.

Critics and press move in and the 'private' experience of making the film together is overtaken by it becoming 'public' property – having to tell anecdotes, explain, quantify and sell the story. Given how close we all were in Swaziland, the inevitable process of having to let it all go is quietly painful.

### 11 September 2005

Opening in Edinburgh translated into front-page coverage and support from the home team.

Checking into the Sutton Place Hotel in Toronto is chaotic – producers and directors from around the globe are crammed into the foyer and anterooms where we are each handed info packs and a Bible-thick brochure of the films to be screened, a zillion of them competing for attention. A Chilean director comforts me with the fact that my film is in English with a recognizable cast, making it 500 per cent more saleable than non-English-speaking films.

### 12 September 2005

Joy Wong reports that MC won't be coming over for tonight's screening, claiming she is too busy. Hallelujah! We shake our heads in relieved bemusement at her last-minute withdrawal.

Press-round at the Hyatt Hotel from 11 a.m. till 4 p.m. There is a holding area on the first floor with a photo studio, make-up salon, hairdressers, DJ, food table, sofas and a plethora of mobile-phone-yakking beauties talking at the tops of their voices to publicists and press, mini-skirting their way about.

Miranda, Gabriel and I are offered free clothes, hair products, luggage, cameras, booze, chocolates, perfume and various assorted doo-dahs between being hustled in and out of various rooms where we get to talk about the film for a couple of minutes. It is as about as removed from the experience of making it as it's possible to get.

As the day wears on, the poor sods having to ask the same questions are looking understandably brain-damaged – what's it about, what's your role, why did you wanna make it? Oh, and any funny stories? Whether your film is categorized as 'small', i.e. independent, or 'big', i.e. studio, the actors are still required to answer exactly the same questions.

Meet up with my old *Dracula* cohorts in the corridors between interviews. Keanu Reeves, despite his *Matrix* multibillion-dollar success, is as friendly and accessible as ever, and retains that 'little boy lost' quality he had fifteen years ago. Then, as I scoot out of one interview, an unmistakeable voice Hannibal Lecters me in my tracks. I turn around and see Sir Anthony Hopkins, flanked by two bodyguards the size of wardrobes, and we catch up as best we can. Knighted, remarried, Oscar'd and clearly much more at peace with the world, it is a real warm pleasure to run into both him and Keanu amidst the dehumanized antics of an all-day press junket.

Limo'd off to the multiplex for the screening, with Miranda Richardson, Harriet Robinson (our mutual agent from London), Gabriel Byrne and actor Ronan Vibert, who is here for another film, and Canadian playwright David Williams. Packed house, and the response is intense and immediate. Any doubt I had about the story crossing the Atlantic and being too bound to a particular moment in English colonial history is obliterated.

Two long tables are set out in the private room of a restaurant for our post-screening dinner. Our gang fill up one of them, including Joy Wong's team from the Works. The producers' table, however, remained empty. A South African executive producer finally cruises in an hour later and joins the end of our table, after we had toasted our absentee 'lords and masters'. Having taken three months to agree on the final credits and billing, it's curious that they haven't shown up.

*15 November 2005*

Joy Wong calls with the Holy Grail of news: the film has been sold for distribution to America, Canada, Australia, New Zealand, Brazil, South Africa, France and the UK, and got a rave review in *Variety*.

We are *finally* on our way!!!!

None of the negatives can ever overwhelm or erase the 500-carat-gold pleasure of making it, or the ongoing friendships that have been forged during its creation. It has quite literally been the journey of my lifetime. Thanks for coming along for the ride.

Richard (E. Grant)

# Credits

I am indebted to all these people, without whom the film would not have been possible. Jeff Abberley, Gordon Adams, Pierre Aïm, Robert and Kathryn Altman, George Amos, Lallie Avis, Chrissie Baker, Flo Ballack, Etienne Barnard, Bunny Barnes, Tom Bayly, Sean Berkhout, Ray Berman, Virginie Berrotte, Sanjeev Bhaskar, Matt Biffa, Julia Blackman, Noel Boisson, Kim Borrell, Kobus Botha, Dave Brackley, Barbra Braun, John Bright, Kate Buckley, Laura Burn, Sarah Camlet, Peter Capaldi, Nicole Carmen-Davies, David Castell, Antoine de Caunes, Penny Charteris, Jean-Michel Chauvet, Annie Christmas, Terry Clegg, Tim Cook, Mark Cooksey, Clair Creen, Liz Crowther, Chris Curling, Richard Curtis, Stephen Daly, Bruno Daniault, Shane Danielson, Zoe Dean-Smith, Isabelle Dedieu, Delphine Desbruères, Busisizwe Dlamini, Helen, Stuart and Mary Donaldson, Abi Doyle, Patrick Doyle, Soretha Du Plessis, Andrew Dunn, Mark Elderkin, Mike Ellis, Bob Fabre, Guy Ferrandis, Richard Field, Melanie Finch, Bob Forrester, Stan Foss, Celestia Fox, John Fraser, Tony Frewin, Laetitia Galitzine, Denis Garnier, Kevin Gibb, Andrew Giddey, Rod Goodlife, Olivia Grant, Vanessa Gray, Simon Greenaway, Jean Greyling, Laurence Guérault, Tony and Zanele Hatton, Teri Hayden, Duncan Heath, Hilary Heath, Julie Heath, Bjorn Hellqvist, Candis Henning, Phuthamani Hlope, Lucky Hlubi, Leonie Hogan, Harry Hook, Beverley House, Dean Humphreys, Greg Hunt, Liza Ignazi, Robin James, Martin Jaubert, Ashley Johnson, Hugh and Barbra Jones, Karen Jones, Sara Jones, Zygy Komasi, Geoff Kemp, Rasheequa Kleynhans, Yves Kohen, Xito Kuazangongo, Pierre Kubel, Kate Ledger, Bongani Ledwaba, Danny Lee, Moonyeen Lee, Coenie Le Roux, Kathy Lette, Dominique Levert, Clare Lilley, Valerie Lindon, Jonathan Lipman, Mavis Litchfield, Sally Longinnes, Théophile Louis-Jean, Nick Lowe, Melanie Lubbe, Paul Lyne-Marris, George and Roxanna Lys, Malcolm McDowell, Andrew McEwan, Craig McFarlane, Elizabeth McGovern, Alan McMenamin, Themba Mahlaba,

Elias Makhanya, Cass Mamba, Qhawe Mamba, Sibusiso Mamba, Heather Mansfield, Carlo Manzi, Nick Manzi, Albert Maphosho, Toni Marais, Pippa Markham, Steve Martin, Johnny and Stella Masson, Tendeka Matatu, Steph and Sonny Mathews, Tebego Matsebe, John Matshikiza, Ishmael Maupa, Marie-Castille Mention-Schaar, Neil Merredith, Cheryl Mitchell, Owen Mitchell, Steve Mitchell, Osias Mndaweni, Albert Mohlaba, Itumeleng Mokoena, Kenny Moleme, Joe Mphela, Michael Mphila, Themba Msibi, King Mswati III, Alton Mthunzi, Sheena Napier, Jeremy Nathan, Mike Newell, Joe Rasta Ngceni, Bhekie Ngozo, Oli Novadnieks, Sindisiswe Nxumalo, Alex Oakley, Djamal Ouhab, Peter Owen, Carlos Paiva, Phillip Palmer, Sarah Pasquali, Eric Pateguana, Cecile Patey, Grahame Peters, Joel Phiri, James Pittman, Lyndsey Posner, Rinaldo Quacquarini, Sue Quinn, Alan Raad, Pascal Ralite, Ted, Liz and Ann Reilly, Michael Richards, Alan Rickman, Dan and Ann Roberts, Ian Roberts, Phil Robertson, Teri-Lin Robertson, Bruce Robinson, Harriet Robinson, Maggie Rodford, Richard Rolf, Hannah Rothman, Etienne Saldés, Jennifer Sale, Julia Sawalha, Vicci Sawkins, Christa Schamberger, Mary Selway, Joanne Sennitt, James Shearman, Brian Shingles, Bebee Shongwe, Mathokoza Sibiyu, Sharon Simelane, Solly Sitole, Melissa Slabbert, Jann and Alistair Smart, Dallas Smith, Jade Snell, Hendrick Spangenberg, Jan Spielhoff, Glenda and John Stephens, Jane and Maggs Stephens, Sting, Trudie Styler, Mairi Surtees-Cameron, Hilary Swift, Meera Syal, Gay Thom, Barnaby Thompson, Jiggs, Jenny and Sholto Thorn, Ashleigh Tobias, Susie Tullet, Magriet Van De Wald, Adrian Van Wyk, Adriaan Van Zyl, Deon Vermeulen, Mphumelo Vilakazi, Jean-Roux Viljoen, Lynne-Anne Visser, Sven Vosloo, Andy Walker, Graham Ward, Joan Washington, Tom Washington, Jack Waters, Charlie Watson, Karl Waugh, Paul Weilland, Dee Whayte, Jennifer Wheatley, Izy Wigget, Kevin Wiles, Janine Williams, Gary Williamson, Joy Wong, Victoria Wood and Tamar Zaig.